Presidents from
Adams through Polk,
1825–1849

Recent Titles in
The President's Position: Debating the Issues

Presidents from Washington through Monroe, 1789–1825
Amy H. Sturgis

Presidents from Taylor through Grant, 1849–1877
Jeffrey W. Coker

Presidents from Hayes through McKinley, 1877–1901
Amy H. Sturgis

Presidents from Theodore Roosevelt through Coolidge, 1901–1929
Francine Sanders Romero

Presidents from Hoover through Truman, 1929–1953
John E. Moser

Presidents from Nixon through Carter, 1969–1981
Aimee D. Shouse

Presidents from Reagan through Clinton, 1981–2001
Lane Crothers and Nancy S. Lind

PRESIDENTS FROM ADAMS THROUGH POLK, 1825–1849

Debating the Issues in Pro and Con Primary Documents

DAVID A. SMITH

The President's Position: Debating the Issues
Mark Byrnes, Series Editor

GREENWOOD PRESS
Westport, Connecticut • London

Library of Congress Cataloging-in-Publication Data

Presidents from Adams through Polk, 1825–1849 : debating the issues in pro and con primary documents / [compiled by] David A. Smith.
    p. cm.—(The president's position)
  Includes bibliographical references and index.
  ISBN 0–313–33175–8 (alk. paper)
    1. Presidents—United States—History—19th century—Sources. 2. United States—Politics and government—1815–1861—Sources. 3. Adams, John Quincy, 1767–1848—Political and social views. 4. Jackson, Andrew, 1767–1845—Political and social views. 5. Van Buren, Martin, 1782–1862—Political and social views. 6. Harrison, William Henry, 1773–1841—Political and social views. 7. Tyler, John, 1790–1862—Political and social views. 8. Polk, James K. (James Knox), 1795–1849—Political and social views. I. Smith, David A. II. Series.
E176.1.P9213 2005
973.5—dc22   2005003397

British Library Cataloguing in Publication Data is available.

Library of Congress Catalog Card Number: 2005003397
ISBN: 0–313–33175–8

First published in 2005

Greenwood Press, 88 Post Road West, Westport, CT 06881
An imprint of Greenwood Publishing Group, Inc.
www.greenwood.com

Printed in the United States of America

The paper used in this book complies with the Permanent Paper Standard issued by the National Information Standards Organization (Z39.48–1984).

10 9 8 7 6 5 4 3 2 1

*To Evan David Smith
and His Mother*

CONTENTS

SERIES FOREWORD

When he was running for president in 1932, Franklin D. Roosevelt declared that America needed "bold, persistent experimentation" in its public policy. "It is common sense to take a method and try it," FDR said. "If it fails, admit it frankly and try another. But above all, try something." At President Roosevelt's instigation, the nation did indeed take a number of steps to combat the Great Depression. In the process, the president emerged as the clear leader of American public policy. Most scholars see FDR's administration as the birth of the "modern presidency," in which the president dominates both domestic and foreign policy.

Even before FDR, however, presidents played a vital role in the making of public policy. Policy changes advocated by the presidents—often great changes—have always influenced the course of events, and have always sparked debate from the presidents' opponents. The outcomes of this process have had tremendous effects on the lives of Americans. The President's Position: Debating the Issues examines the stands the presidents have taken on the major political, social, and economic issues of their times as well as the stands taken by their opponents. The series combines description and analysis of those issues with excerpts from primary documents that illustrate the position of the presidents and their opponents. The result is an informative, accessible, and comprehensive look at the crucial connection between presidents and policy. These volumes will assist students doing historical research, preparing for debates, or fulfilling critical thinking assignments. The general reader interested in American history and politics will also find the series interesting and helpful.

Several important themes about the president's role in policy making emerge from the series. First, and perhaps most important, is how greatly the president's involvement in policy has expanded over the years. This has happened because the range of areas in which the national government acts has grown dramatically and because modern presidents—unlike most of their predecessors—see taking the lead in policy making as part of their job. Second, certain issues have confronted most presidents over history; tax and tariff policy, for example, was important for both George Washington and Bill Clinton, and for most of the presidents in between. Third, the emergence of the United States as a world power around the beginning of the twentieth century made foreign policy issues more numerous and more pressing. Finally, in the American system, presidents cannot form policy through decrees; they must persuade members of Congress, other politicians, and the general public to follow their lead. This key fact makes the policy debates between presidents and their opponents vitally important.

This series comprises nine volumes, organized chronologically, each of which covers the presidents who governed during that particular time period. Volume one looks at the presidents from George Washington through James Monroe; volume two, John Quincy Adams through James K. Polk; volume three, Zachary Taylor through Ulysses Grant; volume four, Rutherford B. Hayes through William McKinley; volume five, Theodore Roosevelt through Calvin Coolidge; volume six, Herbert Hoover through Harry Truman; volume seven, Dwight Eisenhower through Lyndon Johnson; volume eight, Richard Nixon through Jimmy Carter; and volume nine, Ronald Reagan through Bill Clinton. Each president from Washington through Clinton is covered, although the number of issues discussed under each president varies according to how long they served in office and how actively they pursued policy goals. Volumes six through nine—which cover the modern presidency—examine three presidencies each, while the earlier volumes include between five and seven presidencies each.

Every volume begins with a general introduction to the period it covers, providing an overview of the presidents who served and the issues they confronted. The section on each president opens with a detailed overview of the president's position on the relevant issues he confronted and the initiatives he took, and closes with a list of suggested readings. Up to fifteen issues are covered per presidency. The discussion of each issue features an introduction, the positions taken by the president and his opponents, how the issue was resolved, and the long-term effects of the issue. This is followed by excerpts from two primary documents, one representing the president's position and the other representing his opponents' position. Also included in each volume is a timeline of significant events of the era and a general bibliography of sources for students and others interested in further research.

As the most prominent individual in American politics, the president receives enormous attention from the media and the public. The statements, actions, travels, and even the personal lives of presidents are constantly scrutinized. Yet it is the presidents' work on public policy that most directly affects American citizens—a fact that is sometimes overlooked. This series is presented, in part, as a reminder of the importance of the president's position.

Mark Byrnes

TIMELINE

1824   Disputed presidential election. No candidate receives a majority of electoral votes. Decision goes to the House of Representatives.

1825   House of Representatives selects John Quincy Adams to be president. Adams inaugurated.

Adams's selection of Henry Clay as his secretary of state raises charges of corruption from angry supporters of Andrew Jackson.

Adams puts forth ambitious program of internal improvements including astronomical observatory and national university.

1826   John Adams (father of John Quincy Adams) and Thomas Jefferson die within hours of each other on July 4.

1827   Adams defends rights of Cherokees in Georgia to retain their lands.

1828   Congress passes the high Tariff of 1828, known in the South as the "Tariff of Abominations."

Jackson defeats Adams for the presidency.

South Carolina Exposition and Protest published anonymously.

1829   Jackson's inaugural turns riotous as supporters overwhelm the White House.

1830   Jackson vetoes Maysville Road Bill, a high-profile internal improvement project.

Jackson's rift with Vice President John C. Calhoun becomes public.

Congress passes Indian Removal Act at the urging of Jackson.

Religious revivals begin sweeping across America.

1831   Nat Turner's Rebellion.

William Lloyd Garrison begins publishing *The Liberator*.

In *Cherokee Nation v. Georgia*, Supreme Court Chief Justice John Marshall declares Cherokees have an "unquestionable right" to their lands in Georgia.

1832   Jackson vetoes bill extending the charter of the Second Bank of the United States.

South Carolina nullifies Tariff of 1828; Jackson vows to enforce it.

Jackson reelected president; Martin Van Buren becomes new vice president; Calhoun becomes senator from South Carolina.

1833   Compromise Tariff of 1833 defuses the Nullification Crisis.

Jackson begins removing government funds from the Bank of the United States.

Numerous anti-slavery societies begin forming.

1835   Cherokees in Georgia sign away their tribal rights to lands. The "Trail of Tears" begins.

1836   Texas Revolution secures the independence of the Republic of Texas.

Van Buren elected president.

The "Gag Rule" is instituted in the House of Representatives, automatically tabling without debate any petitions or motions regarding slavery.

1837   Panic of 1837.

Canadian militia destroys the *Caroline*, used to ferry supplies from New York State to Canadian rebels.

"Gag Rule" renewed in House.

1840   Congress passes Independent Treasury Act.

William Henry Harrison elected president.

1841   Harrison dies, the first president to die in office; John Tyler becomes president.

Whigs in Congress repeal Independent Treasury Act.

1842   John C. Fremont maps the Oregon Trail.

1843   Whig opposition in Congress helps defeat attempt to annex Texas.

1844   New anti-slavery "Liberty Party" pulls votes from Henry Clay's presidential candidacy.

James K. Polk elected president.

1845   Texas annexed by United States by Joint Resolution of Congress.

The Autobiography of Frederick Douglass published.

1846   United States declares war on Mexico.

Congressman David Wilmot introduces the Wilmot Proviso, banning slavery from any territory gained from the war with Mexico.

Drastically lower tariff passes Congress.

United States and Britain agree to divide the Oregon territory at the 49th parallel.

Americans in California proclaim the short-lived "Bear Flag Republic."

1848   Mexican War ends.

General Zachary Taylor elected president.

INTRODUCTION

If one were to choose any random quarter-century in American history and examine how the country changed over that time, one would find no shortage of examples of radical transformations. In large part, the story of the United States is a history of a rapidly evolving nation—territorially, technologically, socially, politically. Almost any way one could choose, the grand theme of the United States at most any point in its history has been change.

Yet amid all this swirling change, throughout much of its existence the United States can be marked just as pointedly for the consistency of the problems with which it grappled. Slavery as a political problem and the Cold War as a national security issue, for instance, both lasted for decades and greatly influenced every element of American political and social life. In fact, if one looked diligently, one could find times in American history marked more for the persistency of particular political problems than rapid and sweeping change. The twenty-four years delineated by the administrations of Presidents John Quincy Adams and James K. Polk were just such a time. Many of the contumacious issues of Adams's administration were still unresolved and greatly contested when Polk left the presidency.

This is not to say, however, that there was not a great deal of change over these years. There was, and much of it nothing short of remarkable. Territorially, the United States came into possession of the West Coast of North America during this time and added tens of thousands of square miles. It was getting more and more difficult to find someone who had been born when the American states were British colonies huddled along the Atlantic seaboard. Philosophically, the notion of "democracy" underwent a fundamental reassessment and became a positive term rather than a synonym for anarchy. Along with this transformation, more and more people joined in the political process, in so doing both revolutionizing the American politics and bringing closer to fruition certain fundamental ideas that many people believed reached back to the formative idea of the Declaration of Independence.

Early in these years, two of the first three presidents—and the ones most responsible for that Declaration of Independence—not only died, but died within hours of each other on the same Fourth of July. In the midst of mourning, many in the nation believed that they had now entered a new period in their history. In certain ways, they were exactly right. The questions with which the founding generation had grappled— such as whether these states would be free and independent, and what kind of government would the founding fathers institute—passed away with Adams, Jefferson, and their contemporaries. In their wake came the second generation of American statesmen and a second generation of fundamental questions that these men would have to address. Freedom and liberty had been established. Now the question would be, for whom would this freedom and liberty exist? A republican government had taken form in the United States. Now the question would be, whose interests would this new government serve and how would it relate to the individual states?

Every bit as much as had the first generation of questions, these, too, brought with them different possible answers over which people were ready to fight. But rather than being determinant of how the nation would present itself to the rest of the world, these matters dealt more with how the nation would interact among its own people and states. The stakes were high, and people, states, and sections were more than willing to debate, quarrel, and outright fight for the answers they wanted. Already by that Fourth of July, 1826, when the sober news of the deaths of Adams and Jefferson began to circulate, there had been heated arguments in Congress over questions like the tariff and territorial expansion. No one expected that a brief period of mourning would be anything but a short intermission before the fighting resumed.

Despite heated exchanges with scant hope of definitive resolution, many could nevertheless remember a time when harmony had settled upon the political landscape and bitter sectionalism had been quiescent. For a few years, in the wake of the War of 1812, the hope of George Washington seemed to have been realized. The spirit of party, as he had called factional fighting, was nowhere to be seen. In large part, this was due to a booming economy after the war, and to a booming European economy that was finally emerging from nearly twenty-five years of the war that reached from the early days of the French Revolution to the ultimate defeat of Napoleon at Waterloo. Even though many in the United States were proud to have fought the British once again—some even said that "we whipped 'em" again—official relations between the two nations were rapidly repaired by conscientious and thoughtful diplomats who believed that the two shared a common destiny of friendship and economic partnership. Such rapprochement contributed to economic growth on both sides of the Atlantic.

On the domestic front, so harmonious and prosperous were these years that they came to be called "The Era of Good Feelings." Even the Virginian James Monroe, who was elected president in 1816, again in 1820 and who, irritatingly enough to New Englanders, was the third consecutive Virginian to hold the office and the fourth out of five presidents from the Old Dominion, was welcomed with such enthusiasm on his trip to Boston that newspaper reporters were stunned at the greeting. President Monroe now appeared as the symbol of the nation more so than any president had since Washington.

In such a time, no issue seemed strong enough to drive a wedge between states and the national government. As a measure of the remarkable way things had changed since before the war, politicians who had long considered themselves Jeffersonians—even James Madison—in 1816 embraced Alexander Hamilton's idea of a government-sponsored national bank. Many older politicians, surely, were glad Hamilton himself was dead so as not to see them embracing his idea against which they had fought for so long back in the 1790s, but the new generation of politicians didn't worry about such things. A feeling of unity and hope energized the capital city, even though several buildings, including the Capitol, still lay charred from the British army's destructive visit in 1814. Many hoped the nation was at last achieving the goal of the founders of a government with no parties. And it seemed more than likely: If Jeffersonian Republicans could embrace the Bank—and the protective tariff, too—what was not possible?

Even the southern states, dependent as they were on agriculture, accepted the tariff as a beneficial policy. The bulging coffers of the national government allowed it to fund construction projects like roads, bridges, forts, and canals, a nationwide program of what were termed "internal improvements," in every state of the union. Americans were beginning to cross the Mississippi River and settle in the Louisiana Purchase territory, hundreds of thousands of square miles of land that appeared to be just waiting for the American farmer and his plow to bring forth its bounty. By 1819 there were a sufficient number of people living in the Missouri territory for it to begin the process of becoming a state—the first to emerge in the trans-Mississippi. People there and throughout Kentucky, Tennessee, Mississippi, and Alabama were buying up inexpensive land either for their own farms and homesteads or in the hopes of reselling at a big profit. The national government that had made this all

possible seemed to be an unquestionable blessing. States fell in line behind its policies. This really was an era of good feelings, and the good
feelings were directed toward the government in Washington City.

All those people who earnestly and sincerely pronounced eulogies for
the "party spirit" or "factions" were sadly mistaken, however, and it
didn't take long to discover this. By the time the country was ready to
elect Monroe's successor, everything had changed. The economic boom
had ended with a resounding crash and deep depression. Western states
blamed the policies of the Second Bank of the United States and turned
angrily against it. Southern states, faced with plummeting cotton prices,
and therefore profits and their entire economy, were no longer in any
mood to support a tariff policy whose sole beneficiary now seemed to be
northern states. But New England, its emerging textile industry crippled
by the financial panic and depression, now needed the tariff more than
ever. Every state still wanted those internal improvements, of course, but
now there wasn't enough money in the treasury to fund them all. Suddenly, all the states were in competition with each other for control of national government policy and its largesse.

The issue of Missouri's statehood illustrated perfectly the collapse of
good feelings. Suddenly, the potential of admitting a new state into the
union had vast sectional ramifications, and the split that became obvious
involved slave states versus free states more than simply North versus
West versus South. The specific question was whether Missouri would
join the union as a slave state or as a free state. That there were slaves in
Missouri already led many in Washington to assume that the new state
would align itself politically with other slave states. It just so happened
that when Missouri announced it was ready to join the union, there were
eleven free states and eleven slave states, creating in the Senate a perfect
balance of 22 slave-state senators and 22 free-state senators. Now this new
member would upset that balance, one way or the other, and representatives and senators speaking for each faction sought to prevent the state
from joining the ranks of the other. Control of Congress was suddenly
now a prize that each section wanted to win. And slavery had become
the dividing line.

From his retirement in Monticello, Thomas Jefferson said that the fight
over Missouri frightened him as would "a fire bell in the night" and
caused him to fear for the union's existence. Former president John
Adams also believed the issue had the potential to split the nation in two.
Even though there were blatant threats and predictions of breaking up
the union, cooler heads in Congress prevailed, and led by the able young
Kentucky politician Henry Clay, they worked out a compromise. Missouri
would join the union as a slave state, and to retain congressional balance,
Massachusetts surrendered its claims to its northern territory, which Con-

gress then admitted as the free state of Maine. As for slavery in the rest of the Louisiana Purchase territory, there would in the future be no slavery allowed north of the 36° 30' latitude line.

Each side of the issue, however, now understood just how dedicated the other was in its position toward slavery. Many representatives from free states would not accept any further spread of slavery. Just as many of their southern counterparts were equally determined to protect what they understood as their constitutional right to own property in slavery. Over the next few decades, the interrelationship of slavery and representation would lurk behind countless political issues from the tariff to territorial expansion. For now, however, the Missouri Compromise drew down the political agitation over slavery, but most thoughtful observers believed the question was bound to return, given the slow but perceptible growth of anti-slavery feeling in the North, and a concomitant southern defense of the institution that was growing more politically determined from one year to the next.

The financial panic of 1819 and subsequent economic depression, along with the bitter divisions revealed by the Missouri question, had not only brought about a monetary crisis but a crisis of the spirit as well. Nothing quite like this had ever struck the United States, and the severity of it created a deep sense of hopelessness. Little could assuage the feeling. The nation's political leadership, from James Monroe on down, held little promise for any sort of heroic rallying. While he had been popular, he was far from heroic. Few politicians anywhere could meet this description. Where there was once good feeling and unity, now people only saw a dearth of leadership and inspiration.

Into this void of inspirational leadership stepped General Andrew Jackson. Jackson had become a national hero at the Battle of New Orleans in January 1815, and since then his name had never been far from the public consciousness. In one of his more infamous episodes, he led troops into Florida later in the decade to squelch Indian raids into U.S. territory, and in the process caught and executed two British citizens whom he suspected of being involved in these raids. This nearly caused a serious diplomatic problem for the Monroe administration, but it was wildly popular with the people. Later, Jackson served as a senator from his adopted home state of Tennessee. Then, in the watershed election of 1824, he and his backers believed it was time for Old Hickory, as he was known, to be the president of the United States.

Reflecting the shattered mood of the nation in the wake of the Panic of 1819, there were five candidates for president in 1824, all claiming to be Jeffersonian Republicans (or now, simply, Republicans) and all from different states. John Quincy Adams from Massachusetts, who had served as Monroe's secretary of state; William Crawford of Virginia, who was

Monroe's secretary of the treasury; John C. Calhoun of South Carolina; Henry Clay of Kentucky; and Andrew Jackson from Tennessee were the candidates.

The election was a heated one, and in the end, no candidate received a majority of the electoral votes. Because of the Twelfth Amendment to the Constitution, it fell to the House of Representatives to choose between the three top vote-getters: Jackson, Adams, and Crawford. When Henry Clay threw his support behind Adams the dye was cast and Adams became the new president. But shortly thereafter, when Adams chose Clay to be his secretary of state, howls of protest of a "corrupt bargain" erupted from the Jacksonians, many of whom already felt as though the House had stolen the election from Jackson. Here, for them, was the proof they needed. Jackson privately called Clay, whom he already greatly disliked, the "Judas of the West." Over and over they charged corruption. For the next four years, Jackson—and, more importantly, his backers—kept up their drumbeat of criticism of the Adams administration. Jackson's allies in Congress, of which there were many, immediately closed ranks against anything Adams wanted to achieve, while outside the capital, Jacksonians began planning for the next presidential election. In October 1825, just months after Adams's inauguration, the Tennessee legislature nominated Jackson for president again, and he began to collect endorsements.

The entire affair concerning the election convinced Jackson that politics in the nation's capital was thoroughly corrupted, scornful of and disinterested in the popular will, and in dire need of vast reform and new blood. Jackson began to understand his political career as a moral crusade on the part of liberty and the people against elitism, aristocracy, and privilege. Jackson's moral outrage—often over personal issues—would become the hallmark of his political positions for the rest of his life and the lens through which he would view even the most technical policy questions.

The lengthy Jackson-versus-Adams contest, playing out as it did over the course of four years, clearly reflected two of the broadest issues with which the nation was dealing in the 1820s and, more importantly, the issues with which it would grapple for the next thirty years at least. Those issues were the meaning of democracy and the proper relation of the national government to that of the states. On one side was Adams—a man who clearly believed that the national government was constitutionally vested beyond question with the powers to take almost any action that could be justified for the betterment of the United States: for instance, creating a national bank. Coupled with this belief was his conviction that the common people did not know what was best for the nation. Most could not be trusted not to pursue their own selfish interests at the expense of the nation.

Jackson embodied the opposite in each of these two ideas. He was solidly skeptical of centralized power in government, and was not reluctant at all to circumscribe closely what it could do. States had particular rights on which the central government could not encroach, in Jackson's view. So, too, did the common people of the nation. He viewed himself as their representative, elected to do their bidding, more than he saw himself as a leader in the purest sense of that word. In the case of democracy, he was clearly at the forefront of a broader movement that would not be turning backward.

The future of the United States was one that brought more people into the governing process, not fewer. States were relaxing their voting restrictions, not increasing them. The western states, of which Jackson's home of Tennessee was one, came into the union with far fewer limitations on who could cast a ballot and hold office. Gradually, older eastern and northern states were forced to revisit and change their rules, if for no other reason than not to lose emigrants to the new states coming into the union. In this sense, the progress of democratic reform in the United States was set. The question was settled: There would be more democracy, not less. The people's will was to be regarded as the ultimate arbiter of the government's action. And Andrew Jackson fully intended to give form and action to that will.

By the end of Jackson's two terms, there was very little in the way of government policies that could not be framed in terms of the people's interest being the paramount consideration. The leadership style of John Quincy Adams, John Adams, and George Washington was long gone. Now the American president had to speak for the people, appeal to their desires and ideas, and at least make the show of harnessing the government for their wishes. The president was no longer the leader of the people; he was their servant.

The other grand question, however, that of states versus the central government, was far from settled. Even though Jackson believed in the concept of states' rights, and anchored many of his policies on this idea, he was, at the same time, an ardent nationalist. This combination sometimes made Jackson a little hard to understand and anticipate, something that South Carolina would find out at an inopportune time. For all of his sincere and passionate belief in decentralization, he could not let this decentralization lead to defiance. States could not go their own way once the national government had acted in a constitutionally legitimate manner. Doing so, he believed, was no less than absolute treason. Others, however, including some in his own administration, held different beliefs, and although they were well advised to keep them quiet, doing so ultimately proved impossible.

Surprisingly enough, due to the whims and odd currents of the early American electoral process, one of the men who felt most strongly about a state's obligation to stand up against the national government when the two interests diverged was John C. Calhoun of South Carolina, who served as vice president in both the Adams administration and in Andrew Jackson's first term of office. Once regarded as one of the most nationalistic states in the union, South Carolina had been especially devastated by the financial panic and depression, and the little fledgling industries that had sprung up in the state during the era of good feelings were simply destroyed. Worse, cotton prices continued to fall precipitously, even after a broader national recovery had taken hold, leaving South Carolina with the most crippled economy in the nation. Plantation owners, who controlled the states politics, had no patience with government policies that seemed negligent of this terrible fact. The tariff was seen most directly as an economic threat.

By the end of the 1820s the perceived prerogatives of a state in relation to the national government had been philosophically codified in a piece called the *South Carolina Exposition and Protest*. Penned anonymously by Calhoun, it outlined a process that came to be called "nullification," by which a state could protect its own distinct interests against opposing government policies. Following the tariff of 1828, known in the South as the "tariff of abominations," South Carolina was on a collision course with the national government.

Despite the contemporary nature of the specific problem, there was a clear antecedent to South Carolina's dilemma. To a broad portion of the population, a key question that lingered from the end of the Revolution had not been settled: Where did ultimate authority lie? With the state governments or the national government? The matter traced its origins back to the Constitution and had bedeviled the Republic since George Washington had been president. Given their particular situation, southern states were very interested in answering this question in a way that would benefit themselves.

In the North, however, this question of states' rights did not have the resonance it did in the South. Growing numbers in the North believed that the issue bedeviling the Republic in much more obvious and sinister ways was slavery. Since the earliest days of colonization there had been slaves in British North America, and by the 1800s the institution was completely ingrained into the economy and culture of the southern states. Northern states, their economies much less dependent on labor-intensive cash crops, were well on their way to outlawing slavery by the early part of the century. In the South, however, it was more important than ever and in terms of numbers of slaves, growing every decade.

By the end of the 1820s there was a substantial abolitionist movement taking root in the North that began to agitate for the eradication of slavery. Many abolitionists' passions would be fired by the religious revival and social ideas that grew from the Second Great Awakening, and from year to year, slavery was discussed in more starkly moral terms. Abolitionists described slavery as the greatest evil and sin in the nation, one whose existence could no longer be tolerated by a people dedicated to the propositions in the Declaration of Independence. Although their numbers were few at the outset, the tide swelled from year to year. Eventually, they hoped that the government would take steps to end slavery by law.

Southerners rightly saw this as a threat to their society and economy, and the waning of slave-state representation in Congress made them fear for the future. Already the quickly growing population of northern states had caused an imbalance in the House of Representatives. Even with the Constitution's three-fifths compromise that allowed partial slave population to count for representation, southerners realized that the smaller populations of the agricultural slave states would never match the population of northern states with their bigger cities and increasingly industrial economies. Their only hope for political parity rested in the Senate and with keeping the number of slave states at least equal to that of free states. Such had been the source of the heated passions regarding the admission of Missouri.

Clearly, people in both the North and the South could see that for the foreseeable future, there would be new states formed as Americans moved into and settled territories to the west, and that these states would naturally seek entrance into the fellowship of the United States. Therefore, in the eyes of the South, the institution of slavery had to spread westward along with the population. No longer could slavery be defended simply by protecting it where it existed. Slavery might remain in place in the Deep South for time immemorial, but unless it spread westward with the tide of American settlement, slave states would immediately become a minority in the U.S. Senate. In the short run, this would allow northern states to pass high tariffs or any other policy that worked to the detriment of the agricultural South and to the exclusive benefit of the industrial North. In the long run—and this grew as a concern as the decades passed—the loss of slave-state influence in the Senate could provide free states the ability to eradicate the slavery by law or constitutional amendment.

In the relationship between politics and slavery, northern states saw the situation in very similar terms. As the nation moved westward, there would always be the question of whether new states would be slave or free. From this, abolitionists realized that in order to end slavery, a frontal legislative assault on the institution where it existed was unnecessary. As long as it did not spread, eventually the number of free states would reach the two-thirds of the total number necessary to approve a constitutional amendment ending the practice. This is not to say that at any time up to and including the outbreak of the Civil War the North was uniformly abolitionist—far from it. But many other northerners who were not morally concerned with the plight of the slaves did understand that government policies benefiting one section of the country often worked to the opposite effect in the other. The tariff was a good example of this, and as much as tariffs could help the industrial states of New England, for instance, they were fought tooth-and-nail by southern states. Containing the spread of slavery would eventually make slave-state politicians in Congress unable to prevent such legislation, despite their disapproval. Southern states, of course, recognized this too.

There was still another motivation existing in the North to contain slavery and it would eventually become known as the "free-soil" movement. Simply put, northern farmers moving west did not want to have to compete economically with slave-labor farming. Slavery could exist where it did forever, as far as this group was concerned, as long as they didn't have to compete with plantations.

Such was the new style of conflict over slavery that emerged in the years from John Quincy Adams to James K. Polk. Those who opposed it in the North could claim that they had no intention of touching slavery where it existed, and in fact, many who thought this way admitted that the national government did not have the authority to end slavery. But for the South, as the nation expanded, keeping slavery intact where it existed was no longer enough to ensure its future. Slavery had to expand in order for slave-state representation to keep up with free-state representation. By the 1830s, then, the whole question of slavery had changed from its existence to its expansion.

Territorial expansion was a constant in these years. From individuals who crossed the Mississippi River to settle in the Louisiana Purchase territory to merchant ships that made the treacherous voyage around Cape Horn and sailed up the West Coast to places like California and the Oregon country, the lure of land and the promise of the new pulled Americans westward. Out from the line of American settlement stretched a continent that to American eyes was completely unsettled and uncivilized. Thanks to President Thomas Jefferson, the bulk of the Mississippi River watershed belonged to the United States. Thanks to Secretary of State John Quincy Adams, the United States extended its claim westward to the Pacific Ocean, north of Spanish California. And thanks to Providence, Americans believed, this wide-open expanse of land was waiting to be claimed and civilized. For many people, it seemed altogether natural that the United States would someday soon exert political authority from one ocean to the other and that all this bountiful land would come under the possession of the American people.

This fascination with the West, from the Mississippi to the Pacific, finally became a political issue which both parties assumed could rally Americans without any sort of narrow sectionalism. It was a powerful impulse, and by the 1840s it had been given a name: "Manifest Destiny." Magazine editor John L. O'Sullivan coined the term to describe what to him and others seemed to be the providential and obvious (that is, "manifest") destiny of the United States. The Pacific Ocean was the only legitimate boundary of the nation. Americans believed that any other claims to the land were simply not ordained by the steady march of progress.

It was only a matter of time before a president embraced this notion and vowed to carry it forward for the benefit of all future generations. Presidential candidate James K. Polk was the man to do this. Elected in 1844, two of his four campaign promises involved territorial expansion. But ironically, despite hopes that the country would embrace the blessings of this agenda without regard to section, fulfilling the manifest destiny of the United States in this manner brought the question of slavery right back to the forefront of debate and reignited controversy. Would these new territories be slave or free? Would slavery extend from sea to sea coterminous with the land itself? President Polk shrewdly avoided the question, as another of his campaign promises had been to serve only one term if elected. His successors would be left to grapple with the problem, and it would dominate the next decade. Ultimately, it would be resolved with war, the irresistible slide toward which would be the preeminent political albatross around the necks of subsequent presidents who would craft their positions and govern as best they could.

The individual president, however, was often not the only key player in legislative and political battles. The years between 1824 and 1848 were notable for the careers of three men in particular who never reached the presidency but whose stations in the public eye (often in the very center of swirling controversies) guaranteed that they would be remembered and regarded every bit as much as (and perhaps more than) a couple of the presidents during these years. These three were Henry Clay, John C. Calhoun, and Daniel Webster.

Clay, Calhoun, and Webster were remarkably gifted politicians and perceptive shapers of public policy. In terms of political philosophy, Calhoun stands apart from the other two in that, for the bulk of his career, he was the premier spokesman for states' rights against an activist central government. Clay and Webster, on the other hand, consistently championed the notion that the national government's authority could and should be extended much further than people like Calhoun were willing to abide.

In addition to their influential careers, especially in Congress, what distinguished these three men was that they were very often on the opposite side from the president in many of the key issues of the day. Clay, in fact, ran against several of the presidents during these years, and certainly, as a spokesman for the "American System" of government activism, ran squarely up against the tendency of Democrats—especially Andrew Jackson—who sought to limit the national government rather than expand it. Daniel Webster thought in much the same way as did Clay, and although his oratory in the Senate and before the Supreme Court was renowned, his career lacked the perennial unsuccessful runs for the White House and so he was slightly less well known. For a few years, all three were in the Senate, and were widely regarded as the best spokesmen for their respective positions the age had to offer, presidents included.

Henry Clay's political staying power and influence, plus the consistency with which he embraced a few fundamental assumptions about the role of government, made him the very embodiment of centralization and activism, and the antipode to most of the presidents with whom he served in government, with the exception of John Quincy Adams. Of all the political figures in this era, presidents included, Henry Clay ranks near the top of the list in terms of influence and importance. His influence and the political positions to which he gave voice deserve to rank alongside any of the presidents with whom he served. His career in Washington kept him in the middle of political fights longer than any of these presidents, and so he had many more opportunities to shape government policy. Few careers, however, were punctuated by as much frustration as that of Henry Clay. He lost every time he ran for president, and the only Whig elected president during these years, William Henry Harrison, died just weeks into his term and was replaced by someone who was not a Whig.

Clay was the architect of numerous and crucial compromises throughout his career, from the Missouri Compromise to the Compromise of 1850, and such accomplishments spoke to his abilities as a legislator. In all likelihood, he would not have been as effective as a president, so his positions were advanced better, ironically, by his "confinement" to Congress. After his lengthy public service, Henry Clay died in the summer of 1852. John Tyler alone, of the Presidents who served from 1825 to 1849 (and the man who replaced William Henry Harrison), outlived him. The number of times the reader of this volume will come across the name of Henry Clay is testament to the role he played during these years.

No other figure in government, however, has the profile of the president. No other office has the ability—even if it remains unused—to bend the public interest, mood, and debate toward the occupant's own thoughts and beliefs. It is the president, then, to whom we turn our attention when we study the shaping of political debate and governmental action. The president's position has a potential for power unequalled by others in the government. Even in negative terms, as in through the presidential veto, the influence of the office can be supreme. Since few who seek it and fewer who attain it seem willing to let other people set the agenda, understanding the president's position is key to understanding the evolution of government policy.

1

JOHN QUINCY ADAMS

(1825–1829)

The thunderous sound of booming cannon from the Battle of Bunker Hill echoed through the warm June air of coastal Massachusetts. Not far down the coast, listening to the sound with great anxiety, was a young boy of seven named John Quincy Adams. From a hill close to their house, he and his mother Abigail could see smoke rising off to the north from the direction of Boston. They would find out later that day a family friend had been killed in the battle. John Quincy's father, John Adams, was away in Philadelphia at the time, serving in the Second Continental Congress. The elder Adams was well on his way to a political career that would culminate in his being elected the second president of the independent United States. Between now and then, however, he would travel to France, the Netherlands, and Great Britain, all in service to his country. He would serve under George Washington as the first vice president of the United States. Through all these experiences, he made sure that his eldest son John Quincy was involved as well.

John Quincy Adams was born in 1767 and was only eleven years old when the Continental Congress sent his father to Paris to help negotiate an alliance with the French. John Adams took his son with him. John Quincy came home and graduated from Harvard in 1787, and within a few years, his abilities had reached the attention of President George Washington, who appointed him Minister to The Netherlands. After this, his father appointed him Minister to Prussia. In 1802, John Quincy was elected senator from Massachusetts, but because his support of President Thomas Jefferson during the Napoleonic Wars alienated his Massachusetts supporters, he resigned before the end of his term as voters decided to hold the senatorial election early to get rid of him. Shortly afterward, however, James Madison appointed him Minister to Russia and later chose him to be one of the negotiators for the Treaty of Ghent that ended the War of 1812. His lifetime of travel and of diplomatic service to his nation culminated in his being named President James Monroe's secretary of state.

John Quincy Adams thrived as secretary of state, and was a tremendous success at it, one of the most effective the nation has ever had, in fact. He negotiated the treaty with Spain to transfer the Floridas to the United States and also determined the boundary between the Louisiana Territory and Spain's possessions in North America. Adams also deserves credit for the shaping of the seminal policy of American diplomacy that came to be called the Monroe Doctrine.

With his famous name and famous political career, it was natural that John Quincy Adams would someday stand for the presidency. Even though the Federalist Party finally died out during the War of 1812, the booming years following the war allowed for a general appreciation of Federalist principles such as government activism, a bank, a tariff, and internal improvements, to animate the Jeffersonian Republican party. This squared nicely with Adams's own views; he had little use for the states' rights philosophy that had been typical Jeffersonian-Republicanism back when his father was president. But as the party adopted policies like the Second Bank of the United States and an active program of spending federal dollars on various internal improvements, the Republicans came around to Adams's liking.

The office of secretary of state had become a clear stepping-stone to the presidency, with Jefferson, Madison, and Monroe all serving in that capacity before ascending to Chief Executive. This made it seem even more natural that Adams would succeed President Monroe. That Adams was not from Virginia was still another definite mark in his favor as Jefferson, Madison, and Monroe were all from that state and many people from other parts of the country were growing tired of the "Virginia Dynasty," as it was sometimes called.

But politics changed radically over the course of the Monroe administration, and the country's mood in 1824—the year Monroe would be stepping down and whomever was his successor would be elected—was quite different than in 1816. The Panic of 1819 and the economic depression that followed were the cause. The Era of Good Feelings was utterly gone, and each section of the nation was bitterly suspicious of the others. National policies no longer brought national results. What worked to the benefit of one section worked to the detriment of others. Trust between politicians, states, and regions was all but evaporated. In its place was a heated and mistrustful competition for control of the federal government. The Republican coalition shattered apart and as many as five regional candidates were set to compete for the presidency.

Into this bitter and mutually suspicious political mood stepped John Quincy Adams, who, in 1824, wanted to be president. In all of American history one would be hard-pressed to find a worse case of bad timing. Despite his good education, nearly lifelong career as an able diplomat, and record of public service, Adams was not one who had cultivated much public appeal. In this way, he was much like his father, who, as president, never seemed to find in himself the qualities that engendered popularity, or, frankly, even compassion or patience. He himself had little of these feelings toward people with whom he disagreed, and acted haughty and removed much of the time. Many had accused the first President Adams of being a closet monarchist and such epithets seemed to find their way to John Quincy as well. By no means could he be described as having a common touch. He was most assuredly not a "man of the people." And what rankled a lot of people most of all, Adams was perfectly content being described this way.

In many ways, John Quincy Adams was more representative of the waning character of a time gone than of the up-and-coming second generation of American statesmen. Adams's attitude harkened back to a style of leadership that was quickly falling from favor. He was, as his father had been, an elitist in the purest sense of the word. He believed that the quality of education he had and the experiences which he had gained prepared him better than almost anyone to lead the nation. The choice of words here is important: He believed he should *lead* the nation; show it the way it should go and bring it along. Most people hadn't had the opportunities and education he had enjoyed, and as such, were quite literally not fit to lead. This is not quite as derogatory as it sounds to modern ears. For both father and son, there needed to be an elite in the United States from which would come presidents, senators, Supreme Court justices, and diplomats. The "people" had their voice through the House of Representatives, and it was actually incumbent on the members of the other branches of government to check and guide the people's passions. Such had been the attitude of John Adams, and it had served him poorly when he came up against Thomas Jefferson, although Jefferson himself could scarcely be described as anything but elitist.

The elitist attitude was even more detrimental to John Quincy Adams, who, among the numerous other candidates for president in 1824, just happened to face the self-styled champion of the "common man," a striking individual who almost single-handedly remade the word "democracy": Andrew Jackson.

The election of 1824 was a messy affair. Because there were many candidates in the running, no one received a majority of the electoral votes. The Twelfth Amendment to the Constitution stipulated that when this occurs, the House of Representatives must choose the winner from among the top three electoral vote-getters. In 1824, that meant Andrew Jackson, who had received just over 42 percent of the electoral vote and who had also received the most popular votes; John Quincy Adams, who received 31 percent; and William Crawford, who received 13 percent. Notably absent from this list of three was candidate Henry Clay, who finished behind Crawford by less than a thousand votes. As the influential Speaker of the House, however, Henry Clay was in position to determine the next president. Clay thought little of Andrew Jackson, but on the contrary, respected Adams's abilities even though in terms of personality they were worlds apart. Clay put his support behind Adams and the House chose him to be president.

When Adams later selected Henry Clay to be secretary of state, the Jackson faction erupted in indignant protest. Cries of "corrupt bargain" stayed on their angry lips for the next four years. All those who opposed John Quincy Adams either for his programs or because they favored Jackson, determined to make the Adams administration a failure. Adams, however, had ideas and plans of his own, and was as determined to get his programs enacted. He hoped that with the election past, the party spirit could be set aside for the good of the nation. He would be sadly mistaken.

John Quincy Adams had an ambitious agenda for doing what was best for the United States. Few presidents ever entered office with as ambitious a plan as that which he brought with him. Among other things, he wanted the government to build a national university, an astronomical observatory, and a vast system of federally built roads and canals. An ambitious program to be sure, but Adams was as tone deaf to the political mood in the country and the mistrust and competition between sections as he was determined to get his ideas enacted.

States were jealous of their prerogatives and were determined to surrender no ground to the national government. Politicians who were concerned with states' rights opposed Adams's plans not because those plans were elitist, but because they were national. In their eyes, the Constitution had not given the government power to pursue activities like banking and building a university. States' rights politicians, with an interpretation of the Constitution that came to be known as "strict" interpretation, feared that the more extra-constitutional authorities the national government took, the more it would threaten the rights of states. There were few differences in this broad issue from when it had played out back in the administration of George Washington. In fact, the first two parties, Federalists and Jeffersonians, had emerged in part over whether the government had the constitutional authority to erect a bank, and whether the Constitution itself should be interpreted strictly or loosely.

Many issues facing the Adams administration came from this fundamental divergence of views between the national government and many of the states. In terms of formal policy toward American Indians, for example, the Adams administration found itself opposing the State of Georgia over which government's policy would hold sway and if a treaty negotiated by the national government ought to have more power than a state's laws. Even more widely fought over was the idea of the national government building roads, bridges, canals, and other programs termed "internal improvements." In the abstract, such an idea was fine, but practically, funds to build things like this were often limited, and doing so set states against each other in competition. Where these funds would come from represented still another problem, especially in terms of tariffs that were seen as helping one section of the country at the expense of another. The proper direction of foreign policy was still another disagreement.

From 1824 to 1828, congressional Jacksonians—or "Democrats" as they were now calling themselves—did nothing but block and derail every program Adams wished to enact. Incredibly enough, Adams's vice president, John C. Calhoun, worked closely with New York senator and Jackson supporter Martin Van Buren to block most of Adams's initiatives. Meanwhile, the Democratic Party continued to line up support and endorsements for the next presidential election, in which Adams was soundly defeated by Andrew Jackson. In all, John Quincy Adams's administration was, for the president, a frustrating time in which the bitter divisions of the country came to influence every issue upon which the president was called to take a position.

Just a few years after he left the White House, the people of Massachusetts sent John Quincy Adams back to Washington to serve in the House of Representatives. He tenaciously defended the interests of the North against the increasing demands of the South. In 1848, he suffered a stroke while at his desk in the capitol building, and died shortly thereafter, in the very seat of the government he had so long and so loyally served.

AMERICAN INDIANS AND THE U.S. GOVERNMENT

One of the emerging questions of the Adams administration dealt with states that wanted to evict American Indians from land that had been set aside as tribal reservations via treaties with the United States. Southern states, especially Georgia, were very interested in extending their jurisdiction over Indian lands with an eye toward removing the Indians completely and opening the areas to white settlement. Adams believed wholeheartedly that the national quality of treaties between the Indians and the U.S. government flatly trumped any desire the states had to forcibly remove the Indians, either by fraud or force. He spoke out against state encroachments on Indian lands, even bringing up his willingness to use force to protect and guarantee federal government commitments if such a step proved necessary.

Georgia, on the other hand, was determined to exercise what it saw as rightful jurisdiction over its territory. That it made little secret of this encouraged speculators, surveyors, and even some self-serving Indians themselves to design fraudulent treaties and land sales that began to worry the legitimate leadership of tribes like the Cherokee. When, concerned about the future of the tribe and its lands, the Cherokee began to file formal complaints in the federal court system and then sent representatives to Washington to bring their case to the Adams administration's attention, the national government found itself in a growing standoff with Georgia.

In February 1827, President Adams made it clear to Congress that the executive branch had the unquestionable authority and responsibility to enforce existing national treaties over and above any objections that might be made by individual states. What was happening in Georgia—with the explicit consent of that state's legislature—was in blatant violation of just such a national treaty, and therefore could not be allowed to continue unchecked. He ordered the government to take action and warned Georgia that military force remained an option as long as the state was determined to follow its own course. The language of the Georgia law that extended state authority into the lands in question, however, made it clear that it was entirely within the prerogative of state government to govern all the lands within its borders in any way it saw fit. Anyone who lived within the boundaries of a state was subject primarily to the laws of that state and to the laws of the U.S. government only secondarily.

FROM ADAMS'S *MESSAGE TO THE SENATE AND HOUSE OF REPRESENTATIVES OF THE UNITED STATES,* FEBRUARY 5, 1827

I submit to the consideration of Congress a letter from the agent of the United States with the Creek Indians, who invoke the protection of the Government of the United States in defense of the rights and territory secured to that nation by the treaty concluded at Washington, and ratified on the part of the United States on the 22d of April last.

The complaint set forth in this letter that surveyors from Georgia have been employed in surveying lands within the Indian Territory, as secured by that treaty, is authenticated by the information inofficially received from other quarters, and there is reason to believe that one or more of the surveyors have been arrested in their progress by the Indians. Their forbearance, and reliance upon the good faith of the United States, will, it is hoped, avert scenes of violence and blood which there is otherwise too much cause to apprehend will result from these proceedings.

By the fifth section of the act of Congress of the 30th of March, 1802 . . . it is provided that if any citizen of or other person resident in the United States shall make a settlement on any lands belonging or secured or granted by treaty with the United States to any Indian tribe, or shall survey, or attempt to survey, such lands, or designate any of the boundaries by marking trees or otherwise, such offender shall forfeit a sum not exceeding $1,000 and suffer imprisonment not exceeding twelve months.

. . . By the first it is declared to be lawful for the military force of the United States to apprehend every person found in the Indian country over and beyond the boundary line between the United States and the Indian tribes in violation of any of the provisions or regulations of the act, and immediately to convey them . . . to the civil authority of the United States in some of the three next adjoining States or districts, to be proceeded against in due course of law.

Entertaining no doubt that in the present case the resort to either of these modes of process, or to both, was within the discretion of the Executive authority . . . [i]nstructions have accordingly been given by the Secretary of War to the attorney and marshal of the United States in the district of Georgia to commence prosecutions against the surveyors complained of as having violated the law, while orders have at the same time been forwarded to the agent of the United States at once to assure the Indians that their rights founded upon the treaty and the law are recognized by this Government and will be faithfully protected, and earnestly to exhort them, by the forbearance of every act of hostility on their part, to preserve unimpaired that right to protection secured to them by the sacred pledge of the good faith of this nation.

. . . It ought not, however, to be disguised that the act of the legislature of Georgia, under the construction given to it by the governor of that State, and the surveys made or attempted by his authority beyond the boundary secured by the treaty of Washington of April last to the Creek Indians, are in direct violation of the supreme law of this land, set forth in a treaty which has received all the sanctions provided by the Constitution which we have been sworn to support and maintain.

. . . In the present instance it is my duty to say that if the legislative and executive authorities of the State of Georgia should persevere in acts of encroachment upon the territories secured by a solemn treaty to the Indians, and the laws of the Union remain unaltered, a superadded obligation even higher than that of human authority will compel the Executive of the United States to enforce the laws and fulfill the duties of the nation by all the force committed for that purpose to his charge. That the arm of military force will be resorted to only in the event of the failure of all other expedients provided by the laws, a pledge has been given by the forbearance to employ it at this time.

See *Messages and Papers of the Presidents* (New York: Bureau of National Literature, 1897), 2:936–39.

Against Adams's Position

Meanwhile, the laws on the books in Georgia extended the state's jurisdiction over the whole state, including land that had been set aside by the national government.

GEORGIA STATE STATUTE

An act to add the Territory lying within the chartered limits of Georgia, and now in the occupancy of the Cherokee Indians, to the counties of Carroll, DeKalb, Gwinnett, Hall, and Habersham, and to extend the laws of this State over the same, and to annul all laws and ordinances made by the Cherokee nation of Indians, and to provide for the compensation of officers serving legal process in said Territory. . . .

. . . And be it further enacted, That all the laws both civil and criminal of this State be, and the same are hereby extended over said portions of territory respectively, and all persons whatever residing within the same, shall, after the first day of June next, be subject and liable to the operation of said laws, in the same manner as other citizens of this State or the citizens of said counties respectively, and all writs and processes whatever issued by the courts or officers of said courts, shall extend over, and operate on the portions of territory hereby added to the same respectively.

. . . And be it further enacted, That after the first day of June next, all laws, ordinances, orders and regulations of any kind whatever, made, passed, or enacted by the Cherokee Indians, either in general council or in any other way whatever, or by any authority whatever of said tribe, be, and the same are hereby declared to be null and void and of no effect, as if the same had never existed. . . .

Georgia State Assembly; see Theda Perdue and Michael D. Green, eds., *The Cherokee Removal: A Brief History with Documents*, 2nd ed. (New York: Bedford/St. Martin's Press, 2005), 76–77.

Adams's veiled mention of military force being possible against Georgia should it not fall into line was considered inappropriate by some, and hinted at the broader and unresolved question of true authority that lurked behind so many issues such as this. That both sides on the state versus national government debate could make a good case of constitutional legitimacy only made the quarrel more lasting. Tempers were sure to flare once irritation gave way to righteous indignation and jealousy over prerogative. John Eaton, soon to be a key and controversial figure in the next presidential administration, wrote his friend Andrew Jackson, outraged that President Adams had taken the stance he did against an individual state.

JOHN H. EATON TO ANDREW JACKSON, 1827

I sent you to day the Presidents declaration of War against Geo[rgia]. [I]t produces no ferment here; it is understood to be a tub to the whale, to divert public opinion from them. None are so silly to believe that this Civil administration, and Civil cabinets who so oft have denounced mil. chieftains will raise the sword against a sovereign State: the thing is too preposterous and absurd for belief. Will he send his little army of 6,000, they will be eat up before they get to Georga, while the mil'a of the So and west will never arm in such a cause.

See John Spenser Bassett, ed., *The Correspondence of Andrew Jackson* (Washington, D.C.: Carnegie Institute of Washington, 1929), 3:342.

INTERNAL IMPROVEMENTS AND NATIONALISM

Part and parcel of John Quincy Adams's political philosophy was a firm belief that because of its size and reach the national government had a distinctive opportunity—and, in fact, a duty—to engage in various projects that were, for one reason or another, beyond the scope of what a single state could do. This conviction made him look approvingly on many projects that held out the promise of benefiting the people of the union in one way or another. The construction of roads and canals, the building of lighthouses and harbor fortifications, all fell under the broad label of "internal improvements," and with the booming economy in the previous decade, most every section of the country embraced the government engaging in such endeavors. The Panic of 1819 and the subsequent depression, however, caused many people to shrink from this idea because such projects were, in many instances, extremely expensive. Plus, there emerged the awareness that a government-built road in New England, for example, would never be of any tangible benefit to the people of South Carolina. Consequently, any sort of attempt by President John Quincy Adams to put his belief into practice was bound to be met with some level of resistance.

To make matters worse, Adams did not limit his concept of internal improvements to roads, canals, and bridges. A child of the Enlightenment in many ways, Adams possessed a lifelong interest in science, mathematics, and astronomy, and a voracious love of learning. Given this temperament, he had no hesitancy in suggesting the government take an active role in furthering learning in the young nation. In his first address to Congress, he unveiled an impressive list of projects he wanted the government to fund. Moral and intellectual improvements, he said, were no less important a task for government than roads. "The great object of the institution of civil government," he told members of Congress, "is the improvement of the condition of those who are parties to the social compact, and no government, in what ever form constituted, can accomplish the lawful ends of its institution but in proportion as it improves the condition of those over whom it is established." To this end, Adams pushed for the creation of a major national university, more money for exploration and surveys, and an astronomical observatory. For a nation divided over the very limited government largesse, such suggestions were bound to make Adams seem out of touch, at least.

Excerpted here is a passage from Adams's *Inaugural Address*, in which he clearly outlines his belief that the government had a responsibility to engage in public works that offered a wide range of benefits. He tries also to preempt skeptics whom he knows would look with suspicion at best on such notions. In response are passages from two prominent politicians voicing their hesitation about having one section of the country pay for the benefits of another, and, in the latter letter, a suspicion that paying for internal improvements was little more than a political ploy to buy votes.

FROM ADAMS'S *INAUGURAL ADDRESS*

. . . In this brief outline of the promise and performance of my immediate predecessor the line of duty for his successor is clearly delineated To pursue to their consummation those purposes of improvement in our common condition instituted or recommended by him will embrace the whole sphere of my obligations. To the topic of internal improvement, emphatically urged by him at his inauguration, I recur with peculiar satisfaction. It is that from which I am convinced that the unborn millions of our posterity who are in future ages to people this continent will derive their most fervent gratitude to the founders of the Union; that in which the beneficent action of its Government will be most deeply felt and acknowledged. The magnificence and splendor of their public works are among the imperishable glories of the ancient republics. The roads and aqueducts of Rome have been the admiration of all after ages, and have survived thousands of years after all her conquests have been swallowed up in despotism or become the spoil of barbarians. Some diversity of opinion has prevailed with regard to the powers of Congress for legislation upon objects of this nature. The most respectful deference is due to doubts originating in pure patriotism and sustained by venerated authority. But nearly twenty years have passed since the construction of the first national road was commenced. The authority for its construction was then unquestioned. To how many thousands of our countrymen has it proved a benefit? To what single individual has it ever proved an injury? Repeated, liberal, and candid discussions in the Legislature have conciliated the sentiments and approximated the opinions of enlightened minds upon the question of constitutional power. I can not but hope that by the same process of friendly, patient, and persevering deliberation all constitutional objections will ultimately be removed. The extent and limitation of the powers of the General Government in relation to this transcendently important interest will be settled and acknowledged to the common satisfaction of all, and every speculative scruple will be solved by a practical public blessing.

See *Messages and Papers of the Presidents* (New York: Bureau of National Literature, 1897), 2:860–65.

JOHN C. CALHOUN TO JAMES MONROE, SEPTEMBER 5, 1828

. . . I concur with you, as to the beneficial effects of improving the means of intercourse in our extensive country. Tho' it is not the strongest bond of Union, it is among those not to be neglected, to the extent, that the powers of government may go; but I would deal frankly, were I not to state, that the experience of the last four years has shown, that the power is exposed to great and dangerous abuses and that it is supported by many merely as the means of transferring the capital from one section to another, without regard to the nature of the objects, on which the expenditure is made.

See Clyde N. Wilson and W. Edwin Hemphill, *The Papers of John C. Calhoun*, vol. 10, *1825–1829* (Columbia: University of South Carolina Press, 1977), 418.

ROBERT Y. HAYNE TO ANDREW JACKSON, JUNE 5, 1827

. . . But does it follow that any one disposed to afford a moderate protection to American Industry or to enter upon a few great works of National Improvement, should support every measure which bears the name of a Tariff Bill, or Internal Improvement? The truth is, that the Administration, have determined, if possible to ride into power on these popular Hobbies, and as they intend to use them only for their own advancement, it is perfectly immaterial, what the character of the particular measure may be, which they are called upon to support. They have in fact, perverted the whole system of internal improvement, into a scheme of buying up the people, with their own money—while Mr. Clay's American policy has degenerated into a plan for granting to a few overgrown Incorporated Companies in New England an exclusive monopoly of the home market.

See John Spenser Bassett, ed., *The Correspondence of Andrew Jackson* (Washington, D.C.: Carnegie Institute of Washington, 1929), 3:359.

CUBA AND LATIN AMERICA

In terms of hemispheric news in the 1820s, a major story was the vast independence movement that bubbled through the Spanish colonies of South America. Worry that European countries might force an attempt to win these peoples back as subjects led, in part, to the promulgation of the Monroe Doctrine, which John Quincy Adams had been instrumental in crafting when he was President Monroe's secretary of state. One of the occurrences in relation to this ongoing revolution upon which the majority of the American people looked with no small measure of pride was the purposeful way in which many South American countries modeled their independence movements on that of the United States. Reflecting this, some politicians and their constituencies believed the United States had a moral obligation to stand fast alongside these fellow republics. At the very least, many thought that because of their political identities, the republics of the Western Hemisphere had much that bound them together. When the announcement reached the United States of a Congress of Central and South American nations being held in Panama, President Adams firmly believed that the United States had to attend.

Adams hoped that attendance at the meeting would cause South American nations to look favorably upon the United States as a trading partner and institute more liberal trading policies. Reflecting his broader conviction that government action could improve the lives of citizens in innumerable ways, he also thought that the influence of the United States could convince the governments of some of these emerging nations to liberalize their religious policies and institute more religious freedoms for their people. Opposition was heated, however. The old warnings of President Washington in regard to foreign affairs were rehashed as opponents saw in Panama a likelihood that the government would be wildly overreaching in its foreign commitments. Also, there was a suspicion prevalent among southern politicians that slavery would be discussed, and by this time, they were determined to avoid the issue at all costs; least of all did they want to attend a meeting if representatives from Haiti might be in attendance.

FROM ADAMS'S *SPECIAL MESSAGE TO THE U.S. SENATE*, DECEMBER 26, 1825

In the message to both Houses of Congress at the commencement of the session it was mentioned that the Governments of the Republics of Colombia, of Mexico, and of Central America had severally invited the Government of the United States to be represented at the Congress of American nations to be assembled at Panama to deliberate upon objects of peculiar concernment to this hemisphere, and that this invitation had been accepted.

. . . [T]he United States neither intend nor are expected to take part in any deliberations of a belligerent character; . . . the motive of their attendance is neither to contract alliances nor to engage in any undertaking or project importing hostility to any other nation.

But the Southern American nations, in the infancy of their independence, often find themselves in positions with reference to other countries with the principles applicable to which, derivable from the state of independence itself, they have not been familiarized by experience. The result of this has been that sometimes in their intercourse with the United States they have manifested dispositions to reserve a right of granting special favors and privileges to the Spanish nation as the price of their recognition. At others they have actually established duties and impositions operating unfavorably to the United States to the advantage of other European powers, and sometimes they have appeared to consider that they might interchange among themselves mutual concessions of exclusive favor, to which neither European powers nor the United States should be admitted. In most of these cases their regulations unfavorable to us have yielded to friendly expostulation and remonstrance. But it is believed to be of infinite moment that the principles of a liberal commercial intercourse should be exhibited to them, and urged with disinterested and friendly persuasion upon them when all assembled for the avowed purpose of consulting together upon the establishment of such principles as may have an important bearing upon their future welfare.

. . . There is yet another subject upon which, without entering into any treaty, the moral influence of the United States may perhaps be exerted with beneficial consequences at such a meeting—the advancement of religious liberty. Some of the southern nations are even yet so far under the dominion of prejudice that they have incorporated with their political constitutions an exclusive church, without toleration of any other than the dominant sect. The abandonment of this last badge of religious bigotry and oppression may be pressed more effectually by the united exertions of those who concur in the principles of freedom of conscience upon those who are yet to be convinced of their justice and wisdom than by the solitary efforts of a minister to any one of the separate Governments.

. . . In fine, a decisive inducement with me for acceding to the measure is to show by this token of respect to the southern Republics the interest that we take in their welfare and our disposition to comply with their wishes. Having been the first to recognize their independence, and sympathized with them so far as was compatible with our neutral duties in all their struggles and sufferings to acquire it, we have laid the foundation of our future intercourse with them in the broadest principles of reciprocity and the most cordial feelings of fraternal friendship. To extend those principles to all our commercial relations with them and to hand down that friendship to future ages is congenial to the highest policy of the Union, as it will be to that of all those nations and their posterity.

See *Messages and Papers of the Presidents* (New York: Bureau of National Literature, 1897), 2:884–86.

Against Adams's Position

JAMES K. POLK TO ANDREW JACKSON, APRIL 3, 1826

The Panama Mission will probably be taken up in the House today, upon an application for an appropriation to defray the expenses of the Mission. It will be firmly met and opposed in every stage, and will probably give rise to an animated and lengthy discussion. It involves as it seems to me a total departure from that uniform course of policy pursued by the Government from its foundation to the present hour; and is a total abandonment of the sound political measures laid down by Washington, and upon which the country have acted ever since, viz—that our policy is peace, that a strict neutrality should be observed by us between belligerent powers, that we should court friendly relations with all, but entangling alliances with none & c. I am opposed to the Mission in every view which I have been enabled to take of it. It cannot possibly do any good. It may and probably will do much harm if we engage in it.

See Herbert Weaver, ed., *Correspondence of James K. Polk, vol. 1, 1817–1832* (Nashville, Tenn.: Vanderbilt University Press, 1969), 40.

ANDREW JACKSON TO JAMES K. POLK, MAY 3, 1826

. . . I am happy to see that this dangerous project, the Panama Mission, will be met fully in debate; to my mind, it is one of the most dangerous, and alarming schemes that ever entered into the brain of Visionary politicians. One from which many and multiplied evils, & dangers, may, & must result, without the promise of any real benefit that could not have been obtained in a different way without endangering our safety and our national faith. . . . The South America's had our friendship, our sympathies & good wishes. We have ministers with them to form commercial treaties, on the broad basis of reciprocity. In our nutral [sic] situation we could serve them more and better than any other way. . . . I can see in it nothing but great evils, & I hope the firmness of Congress will defeat this wild project.

See Herbert Weaver, ed., *Correspondence of James K. Polk*, vol. 1, *1817–1832* (Nashville, Tenn.: Vanderbilt University Press, 1969), 42–43.

THE TARIFF

An activist national government needs one thing above all else to carry into action its plans: money. Since the days of Alexander Hamilton's leadership of the Treasury Department, a tax on imports was one of the primary means of raising money. During the flush times, such as the years after the War of 1812, the booming economy was so productive that a little extra on the price tag of imported manufactured goods was generally overlooked. With the onset of the economic depression after the Panic of 1819, however, regions and groups especially hard hit, such as farmers in the South, turned against the tariff with a vengeance. No longer were such people willing to put up with higher prices so that domestic manufacturers would be insulated from cheaper imports. The tariff became a serious political issue with sectional overtones.

Gradually, a constitutional nuance entered into the thinking of many who opposed the tariff because of having been injured by it. Tariffs, it came to be seen, could serve two distinct purposes. First of all, they could be simple revenue measures. Such a plan, all agreed, was perfectly legitimate and constitutional. Second, however, Congress could easily design and implement tariffs for the specific purpose of protecting domestic industry by making imports more expensive, thus encouraging people via their pocketbooks to "buy American." Tariffs specifically designed for this purpose, so their opponents believed, were very much unconstitutional. While the Constitution empowered the national government to take measures for the "general welfare," a system of protective tariffs was far from

this. They promoted regional or niche welfare among part of the overall
economy only, while placing the burden squarely on the people who
could least afford it. Regionally speaking, as protective tariffs offered their
protection to American industry, nonindustrial areas of the nation saw
little benefit and much hurt from them. Industries, as it turned out, were
concentrated in the North; there were almost no industries in the South.
Because of this, opponents of the tariff tended to come from the South
and, eventually, formed a key element within the emerging Democratic
Party.

President Adams believed a tariff to be perfectly acceptable, and even
necessary, to enable the government to do what he envisioned it doing.
By the end of the 1820s, a coherent body of opposition was coming together under the intellectual guidance of South Carolina's John C. Calhoun, who worked diligently yet often anonymously to explain the
unconstitutional nature of what was widely and derogatorily being called
simply "protection."

FROM ADAMS'S *FOURTH ANNUAL MESSAGE TO CONGRESS*

... The great interests of an agricultural, commercial, and manufacturing nation are so linked in union together that no permanent cause of
prosperity to one of them can operate without extending its influence to
the others. All these interests are alike under the protecting power of the
legislative authority, and the duties of the representative bodies are to
conciliate them in harmony together. So far as the object of taxation is to
raise a revenue for discharging the debts and defraying the expenses of
the community, its operation should be adapted as much as possible to
suit the burden with equal hand upon all in proportion with their ability
of bearing it without oppression.

... But so long as the duty of the foreign shall operate only as a bounty
upon the domestic article; while the planter and the merchant and the
shepherd and the husbandman shall be found thriving in their occupa-
tions under the duties imposed for the protection of domestic manufactures, they will not repine at the prosperity shared with themselves by
their fellow citizens of other professions, nor denounce as violations of
the Constitution the deliberate acts of Congress to shield from the wrongs
of foreigns the native industry of the Union.

While the tariff of the last session of Congress was a subject of legislative deliberation it was foretold by some of its opposers that one of its
necessary consequences would be to impair the revenue. It is yet too soon
to pronounce with confidence that this prediction was erroneous. The ob-

struction of one avenue of trade not unfrequently opens an issue to another. The consequence of the tariff will be to increase the exportation and to diminish the importation of some specific articles; but by the general law of trade the increase of exportation of one article will be followed by an increased importation of others, the duties upon which will supply the deficiencies which the diminished importation would otherwise occasion.

. . . As yet no symptoms of diminution are perceptible in the receipts of the Treasury. As yet little addition of cost has even been experienced upon the articles burdened with heavier duties by the last tariff. The domestic manufacturer supplies the same or a kindred article at a diminished price, and the consumer pays the same tribute to the labor of his own country-man which he must otherwise have paid to foreign industry and toil.

See *Messages and Papers of the Presidents* (New York: Bureau of National Literature, 1897), 2:973–87 (the last few pages of Adams's fourth address are in Volume 3 of this series).

Against Adams's Position

FROM THE "SOUTH CAROLINA EXPOSITION" IN PROTEST OF THE TARIFF OF 1828

. . . The General Government is one of specific powers, and it can rightfully exercise only the powers expressly granted, and those that may be "necessary and proper" to carry them into effect; all others being reserved expressly to the States, or the people. It results necessarily, that those who claim to exercise a power under the Constitution, are bound to shew, that it is expressly granted, or that it is necessary and proper, as a means to some of the granted powers. The advocates of the Tariff have offered no such proof. It is true that the third [*sic*] section of the first article of the Constitution of the United States authorizes Congress to lay and collect an impost duty, but it is granted as a tax power, for the sole purpose of revenue; a power in its nature essentially different from that of imposing protective or prohibitory duties. The two are incompatable [*sic*]; for the prohibitory system must end in destroying the revenue from impost. It has been said that the system is a violation of the spirit and not the letter of the Constitution. The distinction is not material. The Constitution may be as grossly violated by acting against its meaning as against its letter. . . . The Constitution grants to Congress the power of imposing a duty on imports for revenue; which power is abused by being converted into an instrument of rearing up the industry of one section of the country on the ruins of another. The violation then consists in using a power, granted for one object, to advance another, and that by the sacrifice of the original object.

See Clyde N. Wilson and W. Edwin Hemphill, *The Papers of John C. Calhoun*, vol. 10, *1825–1829* (Columbia: University of South Carolina Press, 1977), 445, 447.

AMERICAN POLITICAL ORGANIZATION AND THE RE-EMERGENCE OF "PARTIES"

Since the days of President George Washington, one of the central dangers that many of the founders perceived to be woven into the fabric of republicanism was the danger of faction. In general, this notion (which sounds rather antiquated to modern ears) implied the existence of groups who sought to further their own specific goals and increase their own power at the expense of the public good. Factions were, in a word, disloyal, or perhaps even treasonous. It was assumed that they would have as one of their immediate goals seizing control of the general government. Few presidents were more wary of such activities, and few more dejected to perceive it taking hold within his own administration, than was Washington himself. It came in the form of Hamilton's supporters arrayed against Jefferson's supporters over the issue of Hamilton's financial plan. Typically, each member of a particular faction believed that his cause was loyal to the government and it was his opponents who comprised the faction. "Party" was a word with scarcely more positive connotation, as it was often used interchangeably with faction. Having little established notion of a "loyal opposition," men of Washington's generation believed that "the spirit of party strife" was but one step away from destructive revolution.

Even though President Adams voiced a hope and desire that the party spirit—that is, in his case, the divisions that had so clearly emerged both in the campaign of 1824 and the aftermath of the election—would prove, as he said, "transitory," it became clear when looking into the correspondence of Andrew Jackson and his supporters that they saw this political strife very differently. While much in Adams's tone was conciliatory, such a tone was notably absent from the rhetoric of those arrayed against him. For Jackson, much of the animosities and collisions of spirit came not from honest difference of opinion, nor even from differing ideas of constitutional interpretation or policy, but from intrigue and poisonous flaws in other people's character. Henry Clay received much of Jackson's opprobrium and suspicion, even before the election took place. Afterward, however, Jackson and his supporters were all the more convinced that such political divides were not going to disappear, but were in fact a bitter gulf between those on one side who were virtuous and looked out for the genuine interests of the people, and those on the other, who looked only toward their selfish motives and those of their cronies.

FROM ADAMS'S *INAUGURAL ADDRESS*

. . . Of the two great political parties which have divided the opinions and feelings of our country, the candid and the just will now admit that both have contributed splendid talents, spotless integrity, ardent patriotism, and disinterested sacrifices to the formation and administration of this Government, and that both have required a liberal indulgence for a portion of human infirmity and error. The revolutionary wars of Europe, commencing precisely at the moment when the Government of the United States first went into operation under this Constitution, excited a collision of sentiments and of sympathies which kindled all the passions and imbittered the conflict of parties till the nation was involved in war and the Union was shaken to its center. This time of trial embraced a period of five and twenty years, during which the policy of the Union in its relations with Europe constituted the principal basis of our political divisions and the most arduous part of the action of our Federal Government. With the catastrophe in which the wars of the French Revolution terminated, and our own subsequent peace with Great Britain, this baneful weed of party strife was uprooted. From that time no difference of principle, connected either with the theory of government or with our intercourse with foreign nations, has existed or been called forth in force sufficient to sustain a continued combination of parties or to give more than wholesome animation to public sentiment or legislative debate.

. . . Ten years of peace, at home and abroad, have assuaged the animosities of political contention and blended into harmony the most discordant elements of public opinion There still remains one effort of magnanimity, one sacrifice of prejudice and passion, to be made by the individuals throughout the nation who have heretofore followed the standards of political party. It is that of discarding every remnant of rancor against each other, of embracing as countrymen and friends, and of yielding to talents and virtue alone that confidence which in times of contention for principle was bestowed only upon those who bore the badge of party communion.

The collisions of party spirit which originate in speculative opinions or in different views of administrative policy are in their nature transitory. Those which are founded on geographical divisions, adverse interests of soil, climate, and modes of domestic life are more permanent, and therefore, perhaps, more dangerous. It is this which gives inestimable value to the character of our Government, at once federal and national. It holds out to us a perpetual admonition to preserve alike and with equal anxiety the rights of each individual State in its own government and the rights of the whole nation in that of the Union.

See *Messages and Papers of the Presidents* (New York: Bureau of National Literature, 1897), 2:860–65.

Against Adams's Position

ANDREW JACKSON TO JOHN C. CALHOUN, AUGUST 1823

. . . I have great reliance on the good sense and virtue of the people, and I hope with yourself that coalition intrigue and management will never place a citizen in the highest office in the gift of the people to bestow. But from the exertions that has been and are still making in favour of Mr. C. we have a right to believe that coalition and intrigue is sta[l]king abroad through our land, with manly strides and the whole exertions of the virtuous portion of the people will be required to put it down. . . .

See John Spenser Bassett, ed., *The Correspondence of Andrew Jackson* (Washington, D.C.: Carnegie Institute of Washington, 1929), 3:203.

GOVERNOR JOSEPH DESHA (KENTUCKY) TO ANDREW JACKSON, JUNE 8, 1825

. . . On [S]aturday last a dinner was given at this place to Mr. H Clay, something upwards of sixty attended and partook of the dinner. It was given in honor of Mr Clay and evidently in approval of his conduct in relation to the Presidential election. [A] number of us, and some specially invited, could not take dinner on such terms, and refused to attend. [S]ome considered it an Adams dinner. The Federal party, or as some call them, the court party, will principally be Adamites, and will sustain those who by management placed him in the Presidential Chair. [A] great portion of the republicans or the party of the people, as it is called, feel indignant at the management practiced. They feel like important rights had been bartered away, but although there is much low murmuring, little is openly said. . . . The management in the late Presidential election will be the tub to be thrown out to the whale for the next season. The party of the people in this state are warm advocates for the right of instruction both implied and positive, and consider, that the man who knows his masters will and fails, or refuses to obey it, deserves to be beaten with many stripes. . . .

See John Spenser Bassett, ed., *The Correspondence of Andrew Jackson* (Washington, D.C.: Carnegie Institute of Washington, 1929), 3:286.

RECOMMENDED READINGS

Bemis, Samuel F. *John Quincy Adams and the Union.* New York: Knopf, 1965.

Dangerfield, George. *The Awakening of American Nationalism.* New York: Harper & Row, 1965.

———. *The Era of Good Feelings.* Chicago: Ivan R. Dee, 1952.

Hargreaves, Mary W. M. *The Presidency of John Quincy Adams.* Lawrence: University Press of Kansas, 1985.

Nagel, Paul C. *John Quincy Adams: A Public Life, a Private Life.* Cambridge, Mass.: Harvard University Press, 1999.

2

ANDREW JACKSON

(1829–1837)

When Americans heard of the great victory at New Orleans over the hated British in January of 1815, it immediately offset the bitter list of striking reversals that the War of 1812 had, until that moment, produced with depressing regularity. The totality of the triumph, from all reported accounts, set even the burning of the capital city into the background. Coupled with the simultaneously arriving news that American and British diplomats in Ghent, Belgium, had signed a treaty ending the war, much of the public perception of the conflict turned immediately. No single person benefited more from all this than the commander of the American forces at New Orleans, General Andrew Jackson. Clearly, people thought, here at last was a new American hero and worthy heir to George Washington.

Not only was Andrew Jackson the victor of New Orleans, he was an Indian fighter as well. Much of the action he saw during the war was against the Indian allies of the British in the South rather than against the Redcoats themselves. Even after the war ended, Jackson continued to lead troops on the wild border between the United States and Spanish Florida, across which numerous Indian raids terrorized settlers in southern Georgia and Alabama. When, in one famous episode, Jackson pursued Indians into Florida and discovered two British citizens in their midst, he summarily had them executed as spies. A nasty international incident for the Monroe administration nearly erupted from the affair, with Secretary of State John Quincy Adams being the lone member of Monroe's cabinet urging the president to actually endorse what Jackson had done with an eye toward using it to gain Florida. Notable among those counseling that the president disavow Jackson's actions was his fellow southerner, Secretary of War John C. Calhoun of South Carolina. All these men would figure prominently in one another's future, and both Adams and Calhoun, who obviously had far more political experience than did Jackson, would soon be overshadowed by the rough-hewn frontier general once he threw his hat into the political arena.

Andrew Jackson was born near the border of North and South Carolina in 1767, and began a law career in North Carolina, but soon moved westward to Tennessee before it became a state. There his star rose quickly, and upon Tennessee statehood, he became its first representative in Congress. He eventually became a prosperous planter and, when the Madison administration declared war on the British in 1812, Jackson joined up and became an officer, a general, and after the war, a national hero. Like many of his status, Jackson was a land speculator in the economic boom following the war. In terms of real estate, few places in the country were as hot as central and western Tennessee, and Jackson made much money. When the bubble burst in 1819, however, Jackson lost much of his money, and, along with others, blamed the Second Bank of the United States for his troubles. The Bank had inflicted this catastrophe on the West in particular to gain for eastern elites the lion's share of the tremendous profits. Through foreclosures, the Bank, at least temporarily, became the single largest landowner in the West. Little more proof was needed for men on whom the intricacies of banking—not to mention international banking—were lost. Conspiracy they saw, and saw the Bank at the center.

For Jackson, this led to a lifelong cause that broadened out to champion the common man against the elites anywhere in society and politics. Capitalizing on his fame, Jackson found himself at the center of the swirling forces of egalitarianism that were beginning to remake American society into one far more democratic than ever before. His fame led him to the United States Senate in 1823, and then, due more to backroom Tennessee politics than to any groundswell of public demand, to being a candidate in the presidential election of 1824.

Jackson took the controversial election results of 1824 as a personal affront. He was convinced that the outcome had been due to a corrupt bargain between Adams and Clay to give the former the presidency—an office that was rightly his, if, like himself, one only counted the popular vote and discounted constitutional procedure. Few men could hold a grudge better than Andrew Jackson. For four years he and his supporters planned the defeat of John Quincy Adams in the election of 1828.

As for formal political opinions, especially on complicated and specific issues, Jackson seemed to have relatively few. He was clearly against the Bank and, one could rightly infer, was against any aggrandizement of the national government's power. He was, in the main, a states' rights man. That having been said, however, he was a strict unionist, and would brook no talk of disunion or secession such as had been mentioned by either some Federalists during the war or by some Jeffersonian Republicans back in the days of the Alien and Sedition Acts. He was uncertain over an issue like the tariff.

For Jackson, personality seemed to override considerations of policy. His fight with the Bank, for example, often seemed to be as much fueled by his intense dislike for Bank head Nicholas Biddle as by any organized and preferred economic ideas. Most of all, he blamed his political opponents for the death of his beloved wife Rachel, and for that, he neither forgave nor forgot. The scandalous turn of events that came to be known as the "Eaton Affair" was still another example of Jackson's tendency to see all politics as personal.

During Jackson's presidency, any institution that stood in the way of the people's will or their freedoms was not to be tolerated. The most spectacular policy fight of Jackson's administration was perfectly emblematic of this belief and serves as a perfect example of Jacksonian politics. The Second Bank of the United States had been chartered for twenty years by Jeffersonian-Republicans back in 1816. Headquartered in Philadelphia, the Bank regulated the national economy and its money supply. Many Americans, however, who did not understand the subtleties of just how a national bank went about its job, blamed the Bank for the Panic of 1819 and for the collapse of western land prices that lingered into the 1820s along with the depression. Westerners who had lost money and/or land—including Andrew Jackson—felt passionately that the Bank was under the control of northeastern commercial interests, and that these people secretly manipulated monetary policy for their own selfish interests. Buoyed by his reelection in 1832, Jackson vowed to destroy what he called "the monster bank" and set the nation back on a course of economic liberty for all. This was the nineteenth-century version of deregulation and embodied both a distrust of the centralized aspects of government policy and a championing of the interests of the common man over the elites of the big cities. Furthermore, Jackson felt a personal animus against Nicolas Biddle, the head of the Bank, and believed he embodied all the special privilege and undemocratic qualities that quite simply could not be allowed to exist in a nation in which the people ruled. Ultimately, through his actions, Jackson succeeded in first preventing the bank from being rechartered and then rendering it meaningless by removing all the government funds from its coffers.

The matter of the people's will also affected the way in which the nation carried on its dealings with Indian tribes. As the population grew, many Americans began to covet lands that the government had formally set aside via numerous treaties as belonging to tribes. Pressure grew for state governments to try to force tribes to relocate away from these lands. Nowhere was this more of an issue than in Georgia where the Cherokee tribe was focus of such pressure. Georgia claimed to be acting on behalf of its people, but found no sympathy from Washington, D.C., until the election of Andrew Jackson. With a president known to be ambivalent at best, and hostile at worst to Indian claims, by the 1830s whether the people's will could trump national treaties became a controversy of its own that culminated in the forced relocation of thousands.

Another standoff during the Jackson administration came with the state of South Carolina over the issue of tariffs. As did all agricultural states, South Carolina suffered under any sort of protective tariff; as there was little or no manufacturing within its borders, a tariff served only to make the goods people had to purchase more expensive. Plus, tariffs fostered resentment toward states that did benefit from such a policy and bitterness toward their representatives in Congress. Slowly, the idea emerged that protective tariffs were simply unconstitutional, functioning as they did for localized and regional economic welfare, and not the "general welfare" provided as a national government responsibility in the Constitution's preamble.

Finally, in 1831, a special convention meeting in Charleston declared that South Carolina would not collect the tariff of 1828 (known in the South as the "tariff of abominations") and that it was hereby nullified within the borders of that state. When no other state joined South Carolina's stand and President Jackson made it clear he would use troops to force compliance with the law of the land, the nullification attempt collapsed and disappeared. Hard feelings remained.

The abolitionist movement began to grow in the North during Jackson's term in office, and although Jackson did not deal with the issue very much, it would be a preoccupation of his successors. The same year of the Charleston convention on the tariff, a sudden slave rebellion increased slaveholders' fears. Nat Turner, a slave in southern Virginia, believed he was divinely chosen to lead a revolt, and he was gruesomely effective. By the time "Nat Turner's Rebellion" had finally ended, Turner and his followers had killed dozens of whites. The militia that captured Turner killed many other slaves. Rumors spread that Turner had been found with copies of the abolitionist newspaper *The Liberator* in his possession. Word of the violence startled the entire South, and made slaveholders all the more interested in preventing abolitionist attempts to reach slaves and inspire in them the idea of freedom.

The years of Jackson's administration were years of great change for the United States. The very idea of democracy changed from being a synonym of chaos to the clarion of self-government. The idea of the presidency as an office that was to be responsive to the people first and foremost remade the way every subsequent president would have to act. From 1829 to 1837, the years Jackson sat in the White House, momentous issues of economics, of expansion, and of the relationship of the states to the national government came upon the country. Andrew Jackson's opinions would lead him into the fight, demanding that his principles, and by extension, those of the people, triumph in the end. In most cases, they did. The president himself was elemental in ushering in these new attitudes, and because of this the president's position would be of central importance in the debates.

Jackson left the White House in 1837, still wildly popular with a great number of Americans. He died in 1845.

THE SECOND BANK OF THE UNITED STATES

Rarely in the history of American politics has a fight over financial policy been so utterly personalized as has been Andrew Jackson's crusade to destroy the Second Bank of the United States. Congress created the Bank in 1816 with a twenty-year charter, and for a short time, during the economic boom before 1819, it excited very little opinion, let alone opposition. In the wake of the Panic of 1819, however, much of the country turned against the Bank, with many people blaming it for the economic chaos that had descended on the land. Especially hard hit by the Bank—through its dealings with local failed banks—was the West. Many land speculators lost everything in the crash and blamed the Bank.

Andrew Jackson's political career was in good part based on his hatred for the Bank and its directors, particularly the aristocratic Nicolas Biddle, the Bank's president, and his image of champion of the "common man" owes much to his painting the Bank as an inveterate enemy of the people and a barrier to economic equality. What came to be known in Jackson's administration as the "Bank War" clearly pitted the people, on the one hand, against the privileged on the other. No greater degree of nuance was necessary, either for Jackson or his followers. He repeatedly characterized the Bank as "subversive of the rights of the States, and dangerous to the liberties of the people."

While such vitriolic rhetoric did wonders for Jackson's popularity, it greatly worried those who believed that a centralized, national banking system was totally necessary in order to keep inflation in check and see to it that the nation's monetary policy, such as it was, was sound. Chief among the Bank's supporters in Congress was Henry Clay, who, more than anyone else, was directly and personally associated with the Bank policy. Since the years after the War of 1812, Clay had given speech after speech on the monetary necessity of a national bank. It had become, in a sense, a symbol of his career, and a symbol of the type of activist government people like Clay and John Quincy Adams believed was absolutely necessary to the well-being of the Republic. That Clay supported it wholeheartedly was one of the few givens in American politics in this day and age.

As Jackson made it a stated goal to destroy the "monster bank," the

Bank's supporters such as Clay worried about rechartering the institution, as its current charter was due to expire in 1836. Clay decided that the best way to ensure its continuance was to force a recharter fight before Jackson stood for reelection in 1832. The excerpts below highlight the two sides and their beliefs. It is very clear that the Bank is more than a financial issue—it had become a defining political position that could reveal how one saw society and its classes.

Against Jackson's Position

HENRY CLAY TO NICOLAS BIDDLE, SEPTEMBER 11, 1830

It may be assumed, as indisputable, that the renewal of the charter can never take place, as the Constitution now stands, against the opinion and wishes of the President of the U.S. for the time being. A bill, which should be rejected by him for that purpose, could never be subsequently passed by the constitutional Majority. There would always be found a sufficient number to defeat such a bill, after its return with the Presidents objections, among those who are opposed to the Bank on Constitutional grounds, those who, without being influenced by constitutional considerations, might be opposed to it on the score of expediency, and those who would be operated upon by the influence of the Executive.

I think it may even be assumed that a bill to renew the Charter can not be carried through Congress, at any time, with a *neutral* executive. To ensure its passage the Presidents opinion's and those of at least a majority of his Cabinet must be *known* to be in favor of the renewal.

President Jackson, if I understand the paragraph in his message at the opening of the last Session of Congress, relating to the Bank, is opposed to it upon constitutional objections. Other sources of information corroborate that fact. If he should act on that opinion, and reject a bill, presented for his approbation, it would be impossible to get it through Congress at the next Session against the Veto.

. . . These and other considerations will induce Congress, always disposed to procrastinate, to put off the question. In the mean time, the public press will be put in motion, every prejudice excited and appeals made to every passion. The question will incorporate itself with all our elections, and especially with that as to which there is so great a desire that it should be incorporated. It will be difficult, when Congress comes finally to decide the question, to obtain a majority against this accumulation of topics of opposition.

See Robert Seager II, ed., *The Papers of Henry Clay*, vol. 8, *Candidate, Compromiser, Whig* (Lexington: University Press of Kentucky, 1984), 263.

JACKSON'S BANK VETO MESSAGE, JULY 10, 1832

. . . It is to be regretted that the rich and powerful too often bend the acts of government to their selfish purposes. Distinctions in society will always exist under every just government. Equality of talents, of education, or of wealth can not be produced by human institutions. In the full enjoyment of the gifts of Heaven and the fruits of superior industry, economy, and virtue, every man is equally entitled to protection by law; but when the laws undertake to add to these natural and just advantages artificial distinctions, to grant titles, gratuities, and exclusive privileges, to make the rich richer and the potent more powerful, the humble members of society—the farmers, mechanics, and laborers—who have neither the time nor the means of securing like favors to themselves, have a right to complain of the injustice of their Government. There are no necessary evils in government. Its evils exist only in its abuses. If it would confine itself to equal protection, and, as Heaven does its rains, shower its favors alike on the high and the low, the rich and the poor, it would be an unqualified blessing. In the act before me there seems to be a wide and unnecessary departure from these just principles.

Nor is our Government to be maintained or our Union preserved by invasions of the rights and powers of the several States. In thus attempting to make our General Government strong we make it weak. Its true strength consists in leaving individuals and States as much as possible to themselves—in making itself felt, not in its power, but in its beneficence; not in its control, but in its protection; not in binding the States more closely to the center, but leaving each to move unobstructed in its proper orbit.

Experience should teach us wisdom. Most of the difficulties our Government now encounters and most of the dangers which impend over our Union have sprung from an abandonment of the legitimate objects of Government by our national legislation, and the adoption of such principles as are embodied in this act. Many of our rich men have not been content with equal protection and equal benefits, but have besought us to make them richer by act of Congress. By attempting to gratify their desires we have in the results of our legislation arrayed section against section, interest against interest, and man against man, in a fearful commotion which threatens to shake the foundations of our Union. It is time to pause in our career to review our principles, and if possible revive that devoted patriotism and spirit of compromise which distinguished the sages of the Revolution and the fathers of our Union. If we can not at once, in justice to interests vested under improvident legislation, make our Government what it ought to be, we can at least take a stand against all new grants of monopolies and exclusive privileges, against any prostitution of our Government to the advancement of the few at the expense of the many, and in favor of compromise and gradual reform in our code of laws and system of political economy.

See *Messages and Papers of the Presidents* (New York: Bureau of National Literature, 1897), 3:1139–54.

NICHOLAS BIDDLE TO HENRY CLAY, AUGUST 1, 1832

You ask what is the effect of the veto. My impression is that it is working as well as the friends of the Bank & of the country could desire. I have always deplored making the Bank a party question, but since the President will have it so, he must pay the penalty of his own rashness. As to the veto message I am delighted with it. It has all the fury of a chained panther biting the bars of his cage. It is really a manifesto of anarchy—such as Marat or Robespierre might have issued to the mob . . . and my hope is that it will contribute to relieve the country from the dominion of these miserable people. You are destined to be the instrument of that deliverance, and at no period of your life has the country ever had a deeper stake in you. I wish you success most cordially because I believe the institutions of the Union are involved in it.

See Robert Seager II, ed., *The Papers of Henry Clay*, vol. 8, *Candidate, Compromiser, Whig* (Lexington: University Press of Kentucky, 1984), 556.

NULLIFICATION

Of all the dramatic episodes of the Jackson presidency, few were as dramatic and full of foreboding as what came to be called the "Nullification Crisis." This episode had to do with the Tariff of 1828. South Carolina believed that the high tariff Congress passed in 1828, referred to as the "tariff of abominations," was abhorrent policy that nakedly put the economic interests of one section, namely the Northeast, over that of others, especially the South. So deeply did certain political leaders in the Palmetto State feel about this issue, and so threatened did they believe their particular economy to be by an unchecked, even unchallenged, program of high protective tariffs, they chose to take action.

What they attempted was not a new concept: Many prominent politicians, even, one could make the case, Thomas Jefferson and James Madison in their Virginia and Kentucky Resolutions of 1798, put forth the doctrine that when faced with an unconstitutional act by Congress, a state could interpose itself between Congress and that state's population, and protect them from congressional overreach by declaring that the national law in question would quite simply not be enforced in that state. It was to be declared "null and void" (hence, "nullification.") What's more, once a state declared a law null and void, the national government ought to have no legal recourse to force the state into accepting the law.

Unfortunately, perhaps, for the South Carolina nullifiers, Andrew Jackson was the president when they tried this. Jackson, while a state's rights man in many ways, would brook absolutely no talk of a state being able to openly defy a federal law while he was president. He equated nullification with treason, and believed that the same punishment ought to be applied to both actions. Over the course of several months, as the crisis grew and played out, Jackson fumed at South Carolina's intransigence. Finally, with his intentions becoming clear, Jackson secured passage through Congress of a bill authorizing the president to use military force to ensure that federal laws were obeyed. Known as the "force bill," its intended target was obvious to all. Becoming just as obvious was Jackson's intention to use it, and any other means at his disposal, to force South Carolina to back down. The tariff would be collected on his watch. Making South Carolina's position more difficult was the fact that no other state stood beside it in standing up to the national government.

Into the tense mix strode Henry Clay, who, with others in Congress, fashioned together a compromise tariff to which both sides could eventually assent. Claiming victory, the South Carolina nullifiers shook their fists at the Jackson administration by declaring the force bill null and void before breaking up and going home. Despite the appearance of compromise, the real result of the entire affair was a defeat for the concept of nullification, and a blow to states' rights. Southern opponents of Jackson complained bitterly of his tyranny and fled the party, temporarily joining forces with the Whig Party and making an odd coalition, to say the least.

The two excerpts below, while quite lengthy, spell out in crystal-clear terms the way each side saw the issue.

SOUTH CAROLINA ORDINANCE OF NULLIFICATION, NOVEMBER 24, 1832

Whereas the Congress of the United States by various acts, purporting to be acts laying duties and imposts on foreign imports, but in reality intended for the protection of domestic manufactures and the giving of bounties to classes and individuals engaged in particular employments, at the expense and to the injury and oppression of other classes . . . hath exceeded its just powers under the constitution, which confers on it no authority to afford such protection, and hath violated the true meaning and intent of the constitution. . . .

We, therefore, the people of the State of South Carolina, in convention assembled, do declare and ordain and it is hereby declared and ordained, that the several acts and parts of acts of the Congress of the United States, purporting to be laws for the imposing of duties and imposts on the importation of foreign commodities, and now having actual operation and effect within the United States . . . are unauthorized by the constitution of the United States, and violate the true meaning and intent thereof and are null, void, and no law, nor binding upon this State, its officers or citizens; and all promises, contracts, and obligations, made or entered into, or to be made or entered into, with purpose to secure the duties imposed by said acts, and all judicial proceedings which shall be hereafter had in affirmance thereof, are and shall be held utterly null and void.

And it is further ordained, that it shall not be lawful for any of the constituted authorities, whether of this State or of the United States, to enforce the payment of duties imposed by the said acts within the limits of this State; but it shall be the duty of the legislature to adopt such measures and pass such acts as may be necessary to give full effect to this ordinance, and to prevent the enforcement and arrest the operation of the said acts and parts of acts of the Congress of the United States within the limits of this State, from and after the first day of February next, and the duties of all other constituted authorities, and of all persons residing or being within the limits of this State, and they are hereby required and enjoined to obey and give effect to this ordinance, and such acts and measures of the legislature as may be passed or adopted in obedience thereto.

And it is further ordained, that in no case of law or equity, decided in the courts of this State, wherein shall be drawn in question the authority of this ordinance, or the validity of such act or acts of the legislature as may be passed for the purpose of giving effect thereto, or the validity of the aforesaid acts of Congress, imposing duties, shall any appeal be taken or allowed to the Supreme Court of the United States, nor shall any copy of the record be permitted or allowed for that purpose; and if any such appeal shall be attempted to be taken, the courts of this State shall proceed to execute and enforce their judgments according to the laws and usages of the State, without reference to such attempted appeal, and the person or persons attempting to take such appeal may be dealt with as for a contempt of the court.

. . . And we, the people of South Carolina, to the end that it may be fully understood by the government of the United States, and the people of the co-States, that we are determined to maintain this our ordinance and declaration, at every hazard, do further declare that we will not submit to the application of force on the part of the federal government, to reduce this State to obedience, but that we will consider the passage, by Congress, of any act authorizing the employment of a military or naval force against the State of South Carolina . . . or any other act on the part of the federal government, to coerce the State, shut up her ports, destroy or harass her commerce or to enforce the acts hereby declared to be null and void, otherwise than through the civil tribunals of the country, as inconsistent with the longer continuance of South Carolina in the Union; and that the people of this State will henceforth hold themselves absolved from all further obligation to maintain or preserve their political connection with the people of the other States; and will forthwith proceed to organize a separate government, and do all other acts and things which sovereign and independent States may of right do.

See http://www.yale.edu/lawweb/avalon/states/sc/ordnull.htm.

JACKSON'S PROCLAMATION REGARDING NULLIFICATION, DECEMBER 10, 1832

. . . I, Andrew Jackson, President of the United States, have thought proper to issue this my PROCLAMATION, stating my views of the Constitution and laws applicable to the measures adopted by the Convention of South Carolina, and to the reasons they have put forth to sustain them, declaring the course which duty will require me to pursue, and, appealing to the understanding and patriotism of the people, warn them of the consequences that must inevitably result from an observance of the dictates of the Convention.

. . . The ordinance is founded . . . on the strange position that any one State may not only declare an act of Congress void, but prohibit its execution—that they may do this consistently with the Constitution—that the true construction of that instrument permits a State to retain its place in the Union, and yet be bound by no other of its laws than those it may choose to consider as constitutional. It is true they add, that to justify this abrogation of a law, it must be palpably contrary to the Constitution, but it is evident, that to give the right of resisting laws of that description, coupled with the uncontrolled right to decide what laws deserve that character, is to give the power of resisting all laws. For, as by the theory, there is no appeal, the reasons alleged by the State, good or bad, must prevail.

. . . I consider, then, the power to annul a law of the United States, assumed by one State, incompatible with the existence of the Union, contradicted expressly by the letter of the Constitution, unauthorized by its spirit, inconsistent with every principle on which It was founded, and destructive of the great object for which it was formed.

. . . The Constitution of the United States, then, forms a government, not a league, and whether it be formed by compact between the States, or in any other manner, its character is the same. It is a government in which all the people are represented, which operates directly on the people individually, not upon the States; they retained all the power they did not grant. But each State having expressly parted with so many powers as to constitute jointly with the other States a single nation, cannot from that period possess any right to secede, because such secession does not break a league, but destroys the unity of a nation, and any injury to that unity is not only a breach which would result from the contravention of a compact, but it is an offense against the whole Union. To say that any State may at pleasure secede from the Union, is to say that the United States are not a nation because it would be a solecism to contend that any part of a nation might dissolve its connection with the other parts, to their injury or ruin, without committing any offense. Secession, like any other revolutionary act, may be morally justified by the extremity of oppression; but to call it a constitutional right, is confounding the meaning of terms, and can only be done through gross error, or to deceive those who are willing to assert a right, but would pause before they made a revolution, or incur the penalties consequent upon a failure.

. . . Fellow-citizens of my native State! let me not only admonish you, as the first magistrate of our common country, not to incur the penalty of its laws, but use the influence that a father would over his children whom he saw rushing to a certain ruin. In that paternal language, with that paternal feeling, let me tell you, my countrymen, that you are deluded by men who are either deceived themselves or wish to deceive you. Mark under what pretenses you have been led on to the brink of insurrection and treason on which you stand! . . . You were told that this opposition might be peaceably—might be constitutionally made—that you might enjoy all the advantages of the Union and bear none of its burdens. Eloquent appeals to your passions, to your State pride, to your native courage, to your sense of real injury, were used to prepare you for the period when the mask which concealed the hideous features of DISUNION should be taken off.

. . . [T]he dictates of a high duty oblige me solemnly to announce that you cannot succeed. The laws of the United States must be executed. I have no discretionary power on the subject—my duty is emphatically pronounced in the Constitution. Those who told you that you might peaceably prevent their execution, deceived you—they could not have been deceived themselves. They know that a forcible opposition could alone prevent the execution of the laws, and they know that such opposition must be repelled. Their object is disunion, but be not deceived by names; disunion, by armed force, is TREASON. Are you really ready to incur its guilt? If you are, on the head of the instigators of the act be the dreadful consequences—on their heads be the dishonor, but on yours may fall the punishment—on your unhappy State will inevitably fall all the evils of the conflict you force upon the government of your country. It cannot accede to the mad project of disunion, of which you would be the first victims—its first magistrate cannot, if he would, avoid the performance of his duty—the consequence must be fearful for you, distressing to your fellow-citizens here, and to the friends of good government throughout the world. . . . You may disturb [the nation's] peace—you may interrupt the course of its prosperity—you may cloud its reputation for stability—but its tranquility will be restored, its prosperity will return, and the stain upon its national character will be transferred and remain an eternal blot on the memory of those who caused the disorder.

See http://www.yale.edu/lawweb/avalon/presiden/proclamations/jack01.htm.

AMERICAN INDIANS AND THE U.S. GOVERNMENT

By the time of Andrew Jackson's presidency, the question of Indian lands being coveted by white settlers, especially in Georgia, had become a burning issue. White Georgians wanted the state to extinguish Indian claims to large parts of the state, claims that went back to treaties signed between the U.S. government and various Indian tribes. Crooked surveyors, fraudulent treaties, underhanded dealings were all commonplace as the state of Georgia sought to move these tribes westward, out across the Mississippi River, where they would be of no trouble to anyone.

Even though Georgia was in a sense trying to abrogate a treaty signed by the United States, Andrew Jackson did not see this as being as threatening to national government sovereignty nor as tantamount to treason as he did the actions of South Carolina in the Nullification Crisis. This is perhaps due to Jackson's own antipathy toward Indians, his gracious language in his speeches notwithstanding. At any rate, Jackson had no trouble whatsoever forcing the Indians to leave their homes and trek westward to parts unknown. Jackson's policy also in a sense ran contrary to that of the Supreme Court which had made clear the treaties signed by the tribes and the United States had legal standing above state laws. Jackson's remark that Supreme Court Justice John Marshall "has made his decision, now let him carry it out," is in all probability apocryphal, but in a real way sums up the president's willingness, in this case, to see a state take action against a national policy. Again, as in so many other of his actions, Jackson enraged his political opponents who railed against what they saw as nothing short of tyranny.

Contrary to Jackson's beliefs, many in America were beginning to see in the patterns of unfair dealings with the Indians a shameful pattern of inhumane treatment and exploitation. Of the many reform movements that caught fire in the 1830s, Indian Removal and the manifest injustice associated with it was high on the list. Societies formed to speak up for the Indians and their fight to stay on their ancestral homelands, and some were vociferous enough to catch the ears of members of Congress, spurring some there to boldly speak out against national policy.

FROM JACKSON'S *SECOND ANNUAL MESSAGE TO CONGRESS*, DECEMBER 6, 1830

... It gives me pleasure to announce to Congress that the benevolent policy of the Government, steadily pursued for nearly 30 years, in relation to the removal of the Indians beyond the white settlements is approaching to a happy consummation.

... The consequences of a speedy removal will be important to the United States, to individual States, and to the Indians themselves. . . . It will separate the Indians from immediate contact with settlements of whites; free them from the power of the States; enable them to pursue happiness in their own way and under their own rude institutions; will retard the progress of decay, which is lessening their numbers, and perhaps cause them gradually, under the protection of the Government and through the influence of good counsels, to cast off their savage habits and become an interesting, civilized, and Christian community.

... Toward the aborigines of the country no one can indulge a more friendly feeling than myself, or would go further in attempting to reclaim them from their wandering habits and make them a happy, prosperous people. . . . These treaties, being probably the last which will ever be made with them, are characterized by great liberality on the part of the Government. They give the Indians a liberal sum in consideration of their removal, and comfortable subsistence on their arrival at their new homes. If it be their real interest to maintain a separate existence, they will there be at liberty to do so without the inconveniences and vexations to which they would unavoidably have been subject in Alabama and Mississippi.

Humanity has often wept over the fate of the aborigines of this country, and Philanthropy has been long busily employed in devising means to avert it, but its progress has never for a moment been arrested, and one by one have many powerful tribes disappeared from the earth. To follow to the tomb the last of his race and to tread on the graves of extinct nations excite melancholy reflections. But true philanthropy reconciles the mind to these vicissitudes as it does to the extinction of one generation to make room for another. In the monuments and fortifications of an unknown people, spread over the extensive regions of the West, we behold the memorials of a once powerful race, which was exterminated of has disappeared to make room for the existing savage tribes. Nor is there any thing in this which, upon a comprehensive view of the general interests of the human race, is to be regretted. Philanthropy could not wish to see this continent restored to the condition in which it was found by our fore-fathers. What good man would prefer a country covered with forests and ranged by a few thousand savages to our extensive Republic, studded with cities, towns, and prosperous farms, embellished with all the improvements which art can devise or industry execute, occupied by more than 12,000,000 happy people, and filled with all the blessings of liberty, civilization, and religion?

. . . Can it be cruel in this Government when, by events which it can not control, the Indian is made discontented in his ancient home to purchase his lands, to give him a new and extensive territory, to pay the expense of his removal, and support him a year in his new abode? How many thousands of our own people would gladly embrace the opportunity of removing to the West on such conditions! If the offers made to the Indians were extended to them, they would be hailed with gratitude and joy.

. . . May we not hope, therefore, that all good citizens, and none more zealously than those who think the Indians oppressed by subjection to the laws of the States, will unite in attempting to open the eyes of those children of the forest to their true condition, and by a speedy removal to relieve them from all the evils, real or imaginary, present or prospective, with which they may be supposed to be threatened.

See *Messages and Papers of the Presidents* (New York: Bureau of National Literature, 1897), 3:1063–92.

Against Jackson's Position

SENATOR THEODORE FRELINGHUYSEN, SPEECH IN THE SENATE, APRIL 9, 1830

. . . I now proceed to the discussion of those principles which, in my humble judgment, fully and clearly sustain the claims of the Indians to all their political and civil rights, as by them asserted. And here, I insist that, by immemorial possession, as the original tenants of the soil, they hold a title beyond and superior to the British Crown and her colonies, and to all adverse pretensions of our confederation and subsequent Union.

God, in his providence, planted these tribes on this Western continent, so far as we know, before Great Britain herself had a political existence. I believe, sir, it is not now seriously denied that the Indians are men, endowed with kindred faculties and powers with ourselves; that they have a place in human sympathy, and are justly entitled to a share in the common bounties of a benignant Providence. And, with this conceded, I ask in what code of the law of nations, or by what process of abstract deduction, their rights have been extinguished?

Where is the decree or ordinance that has stripped these early and first lords of the soil? Sir, no record of such measure can be found. And I might triumphantly rest the hopes of these feeble fragments of once great nations upon this impregnable foundation. However mere human policy, or the law of power, or the tyrant's plea of expediency, may have found it convenient at any or in all times to recede from the unchangeable principles of eternal justice, no argument can shake the political maxim, that, where the Indian always has been, he enjoys an absolute right still to be, in the free exercise of his own modes of thought, government, and conduct.

In the light of natural law, can a reason for a distinction exist in the mode of enjoying that which is my own? If I use it for hunting, may another take it because he needs it for agriculture? I am aware that some writers have, by a system of artificial reasoning, endeavored to justify, or rather excuse the encroachments made upon Indian territory; and they denominate these abstractions the law of nations, and, in this ready way, the question is despatched. Sir, as we trace the sources of this law, we find its authority to depend either upon the conventions or common consent of nations. And when, permit me to inquire, were the Indian tribes ever consulted on the establishment of such a law? Whoever represented them or their interests in any Congress of nations, to confer upon the public rules of intercourse, and the proper foundations of dominion and property? The plain matter of fact is, that all these partial doctrines have resulted from the selfish plans and pursuits of more enlightened nations; and it is not matter for any great wonder, that they should so largely partake of a mercenary and exclusive spirit toward the claims of the Indians.

It is, however, admitted, sir, that, when the increase of population and the wants of mankind demand the cultivation of the earth, a duty is thereby devolved upon the proprietors of large and uncultivated regions, of devoting them to such useful purposes. But such appropriations are to be obtained by fair contract, and for reasonable compensation. It is, in such a case, the duty of the proprietor to sell: we may properly address his reason to induce him; but we cannot rightfully compel the cession his lands, or take them by violence, if his consent be withheld.

. . . Do the obligations of justice change with the color of the skin? Is it one of the prerogatives of the white man, that he may disregard the dictates of moral principles, when an Indian shall be concerned? No, sir. In that severe and impartial scrutiny which futurity will cast over this subject, the righteous award will be, that those very causes which are now pleaded for the relaxed enforcement of the rules of equity, urged upon us not only a rigid execution of the highest justice, to the very letter, but claimed at our hands a generous and magnanimous policy.

Standing here, then, on this unshaken basis, how is it possible that even a shadow of claim to soil, or jurisdiction, can be derived, by forming a collateral issue between the State of Georgia and the General Government? Her complaint is made against the United States, for encroachments on her sovereignty. Sir, the Cherokees are no parties to this issue; they have no part in this controversy. They hold by better title than either Georgia or the Union. They have nothing to do with State sovereignty, or United States, sovereignty. They are above and beyond both. True, sir, they have made treaties with both, but not to acquire title or jurisdiction; these they had before—ages before the evil hour to them, when their white brothers fled to them for an asylum. They treated to secure protection and guarantee for subsisting powers and privileges; and so far as those conventions raise obligations, they are willing to meet, and always have met, and faithfully performed them; and now expect from a great people, the like fidelity to plighted covenants.

See *Debates and Proceedings of Congress,* 21st Cong., 1st Sess., vol. 6, pt. 1, columns 309–20.

THE "SPOILS SYSTEM"

Of all the ways Andrew Jackson set precedents for a president enraging his opposition from the moment he took the oath of office, few seemed to be so naked a power grab as Jackson's policy toward those who held office when he became president. A severe housecleaning was on his agenda, both to remove from positions of authority those whom the president thought would be disloyal to him and to put into positions those people who had worked hard for Jackson's election. This policy of rotating civil servants into and out of office based on who the president was came to be known by Jackson's opponents as the "spoils system," as in "to the victor belong the spoils of the enemy," in the ill-advised words of New York Jacksonian William Marcy. Jackson, who clearly saw political rivalries as something akin to combat, wanted those who had held positions under previous presidents to vacate their jobs at once, so he could bring in his people. He called the policy simply "rotation in office."

Opponents of this policy were outraged at the idea. Nothing could act to bring more incompetency into government, they believed, not to mention the widespread corruption that such an obvious handing out of favors could create.

Despite protests and worries over the very future of republican government, Jackson in fact did not dismiss all that many people from office. In the first year and a half of his administration, he removed only 919 people out of over 10,000 federal employees. It was his attitude, however, that rankled people the most.

FROM JACKSON'S *FIRST ANNUAL MESSAGE TO CONGRESS*, DECEMBER 8, 1829

. . . There are, perhaps, few men who can for any great length of time enjoy office and power without being more or less under the influence of feelings unfavorable to the faithful discharge of their public duties. Their integrity may be proof against improper considerations immediately addressed to themselves, but they are apt to acquire a habit of looking with indifference upon the public interests and of tolerating conduct from which an unpracticed man would revolt. Office is considered as a species of property, and government rather as a means of promoting individual interests than as an instrument created solely for the service of the people. Corruption in some and in others a perversion of correct feelings and principles divert government from its legitimate ends and make it an engine for the support of the few at the expense of the many. The duties of all public officers are, or at least admit of being made, so plain and simple that men of intelligence may readily qualify themselves for their performance; and I can not but believe that more is lost by the long continuance of men in office than is generally to be gained by their experience. I submit, therefore, to your consideration whether the efficiency of the Government would not be promoted and official industry and integrity better secured by a general extension of the law which limits appointments to four years.

In a country where offices are created solely for the benefit of the people no one man has any more intrinsic right to official station than another. Offices were not established to give support to particular men at the public expense. No individual wrong is, therefore, done by removal, since neither appointment to nor continuance in office is a matter of right. The incumbent became an officer with a view to public benefits, and when these require his removal they are not to be sacrificed to private interests. It is the people, and they alone, who have a right to complain when a bad officer is substituted for a good one. He who is removed has the same means of obtaining a living that are enjoyed by the millions who never held office.

See *Messages and Papers of the Presidents* (New York: Bureau of National Literature, 1897), 3:1005–25.

HENRY CLAY, "FOWLER'S GARDEN SPEECH," LEXINGTON, KENTUCKY, MAY 16, 1829

. . . I will not dwell on the injustice and individual distress which are the necessary consequences of these acts of authority. Man who accepted public employments entered on them with the implied understanding that they would be retained as long as they continued to discharge their duties to the public honestly, ably, and assiduously. All their private arrangements are made accordingly. To be dismissed, without fault, and with trial; to be expelled, with their families, without the means of support, and, in some instances, disqualified by age or by official habits from the pursuit of any other business; and all this to be done upon the will of one man, in a free government, was surely intolerable oppression.

Our institutions proclaim, reason enjoins, and conscience requires, that every freeman shall exercise the elective franchise freely and independently: and that, among the candidates for his suffrage, he shall fearlessly bestow it upon him who will best advance the interests of his country. The presumption is that this is always done, unless the contrary appear. But, if the consequence of such a performance of patriotic duty is to be punishment; if an honest and sincere preference of A to J is to be treated as a crime, then our dearest privilege is a mockery, and our institutions are snares.

. . . One of the worst consequences of the introduction of this tenure of public office will be, should it be permanently adopted, to substitute for a system of responsibility, founded upon the ability and integrity with which public officers discharge their duties to the community, a system of universal rapacity. Incumbents, feeling the instability of their situations, and knowing their liability to periodic removals, at short terms, without any regard to the manner in which they have executed their trusts, will be disposed to make the most of their uncertain offices, whilst they hold them. And hence we may expect innumerable cases of fraud, peculation, and corruption.

. . . We may worship God according to the dictates of our own consciences. No man's right in that respect can be called into question. The Constitution secures it. Public officers are happily . . . alike accessible to all, Protestants and Catholics, and to every denomination of each. But if our homage is not paid to a mortal, we are liable to a punishment which an erroneous worship of God does not bring upon us. Those public officers, it seems, who have failed to exhibit their devotion to that mortal, are to be visited by all the punishment which he can inflict, in virtue of laws, the execution of which was committed to his hands for the public good, and not to subserve his private purposes.

See Robert Seager II, ed., *The Papers of Henry Clay*, vol. 8, *Candidate Compromiser, Whig* (Lexington: University Press of Kentucky, 1984), 45, 51.

INTERNAL IMPROVEMENTS

As far as the debate over the national government spending money on internal improvements, President Jackson seemed by and large opposed. By his reasoning, and that of others who felt as he did, a government that spent on internal improvements was a government that gathered to itself more powers than constitutionally allowed. Internal improvements, the construction of roads, for instance, was a duty of the states themselves. Even though the government had, in the past, constructed some toll roads and engaged in other projects that could rightly be considered "internal improvements," Jackson believed that unless such a project crossed state boundaries and could be shown to have a distinct and definite *national* character that existed above and beyond any *state* character, it was constitutionally irresponsible for the national government to get involved.

For projects such as the Maysville Road, which Jackson vetoes in the passage reprinted below, its location in the state of Kentucky cannot be removed from the equation. Kentucky was Henry Clay's state, and the personal element that Jackson injected into all of his politics has to have weighed on his decision, even if it simply lent an energetic confirmation to what he was already predisposed to do. Clay, however, defended the Maysville Road as a project that would, in fact, have national effects, as it would link up with other existing roads, in other states, contributing to the creating of a transportation network that would tie all parts of the Ohio valley together.

JACKSON'S VETO MESSAGE, MAY 27, 1830

... The constitutional power of the Federal Government to construct or promote works of internal improvement presents itself in two points of view—the first as bearing upon the sovereignty of the States within whose limits their execution is contemplated, if jurisdiction of the territory which they may occupy be claimed as necessary to their preservation and use; the second as asserting the simple right to appropriate money from the National Treasury in aid of such works when undertaken by State authority, surrendering the claim of jurisdiction. In the first view the question of power is an open one, and can be decided without the embarrassments attending the other, arising from the practice of the Government. Although frequently and strenuously attempted, the power to this extent has never been exercised by the Government in a single instance. It does not, in my opinion, possess it; and no bill, therefore, which admits it can receive my official sanction.

... The bill before me does not call for a more definite opinion upon the particular circumstances which will warrant appropriations of money by Congress to aid works of internal improvement, for although the extension of the power to apply money beyond that of carrying into effect the object for which it is appropriated has, as we have seen, been long claimed and exercised by the Federal Government, yet such grants have always been professedly under the control of the general principle that the works which might be thus aided should be "of a general, not local, national, not State," character. A disregard of this distinction would of necessity lead to the subversion of the federal system. That even this is an unsafe one, arbitrary in its nature, and liable, consequently, to great abuses, is too obvious to require the confirmation of experience. It is, however, sufficiently definite and imperative to my mind to forbid my approbation of any bill having the character of the one under consideration. I have given to its provisions all the reflection demanded by a just regard for the interests of those of our fellow-citizens who have desired its passage, and by the respect which is due to a coordinate branch of the Government, but I am not able to view it in any other light than as a measure of purely local character; or, if it can be considered national, that no further distinction between the appropriate duties of the General and State Governments need be attempted, for there can be no local interest that may not with equal propriety be denominated national. It has no connection with any established system of improvements; is exclusively within the limits of a State, starting at a point on the Ohio River and running out 60 miles to an interior town, and even as far as the State is interested conferring partial instead of general advantages.

. . . But although I might not feel it to be my official duty to interpose the Executive veto to the passage of a bill appropriating money for the construction of such works as are authorized by the States and are national in their character, I do not wish to be understood as expressing an opinion that it is expedient at this time for the General Government to embark in a system of this kind; and anxious that my constituents should be possessed of my views on this as well as on all other subjects which they have committed to my discretion, I shall state them frankly and briefly. Besides many minor considerations, there are two prominent views of the subject which have made a deep impression upon my mind, which, I think, are well entitled to your serious attention, and will, I hope, be maturely weighed by the people.

. . . Through the favor of an overruling and indulgent Providence our country is blessed with general prosperity and our citizens exempted from the pressure of taxation, which other less favored portions of the human family are obliged to bear. . . . [B]ut have we a right to calculate on the same cheerful acquiescence when it is known that the necessity for their continuance would cease were it not for irregular, improvident, and unequal appropriations of the public funds? Will not the people demand, as they have a right to do, such a prudent system of expenditure as will pay the debts of the Union and authorize the reduction of every tax to as low a point as the wise observance of the necessity to protect that portion of our manufactures and labor whose prosperity is essential to our national safety and independence will allow? When the national debt is paid, the duties upon those articles which we do not raise may be repealed with safety, and still leave, I trust, without oppression to any section of the country, an accumulating surplus fund, which may be beneficially applied to some well-digested system of improvement.

. . . In the other view of the subject, and the only remaining one which it is my intention to present at this time, is involved the expediency of embarking in a system of internal improvement without a previous amendment of the Constitution explaining and defining the precise powers of the Federal Government over it. Assuming the right to appropriate money to aid in the construction of national works to be warranted by the cotemporaneous and continued exposition of the Constitution, its insufficiency for the successful prosecution of them must be admitted by all candid minds. If we look to usage to define the extent of the right, that will be found so variant and embracing so much that has been overruled as to involve the whole subject in great uncertainty and to render the execution of our respective duties in relation to it replete with difficulty and embarrassment. It is in regard to such works and the acquisition of additional territory that the practice obtained its first footing. In most, if not all, other disputed questions of appropriation the construction of the Constitution may be regarded as unsettled if the right to apply money in the enumerated cases is placed on the ground of usage.

. . . If different impressions are entertained in any quarter; if it is expected that the people of this country, reckless of their constitutional obligations, will prefer their local interest to the principles of the Union, such expectations will in the end be disappointed; or if it be not so, then indeed has the world but little to hope from the example of free government. When an honest observance of constitutional compacts can not be obtained from communities like ours, it need not be anticipated elsewhere, and the cause in which there has been so much martyrdom, and from which so much was expected by the friends of liberty, may be abandoned, and the degrading truth that man is unfit for self-government admitted. And this will be the case if *expediency* be made a rule of construction in interpreting the Constitution. Power in no government could desire a better shield for the insidious advances which it is ever ready to make upon the checks that are designed to restrain its action.

See *Messages and Papers of the Presidents* (New York: Bureau of National Literature, 1897), 3:1046–56.

HENRY CLAY DEFENDING THE MAYSVILLE ROAD BILL, JULY 22, 1830, SPEECH AT COLUMBUS, OHIO, REPRINTED IN THE CINCINNATI *AMERICAN*, AUGUST, 5, 1830

. . . Of all parts of the Union, the West is most deeply interested in the prosecution of Internal Improvements. This resulted from its interior situation and remoteness from the sea. Without them, the West could not participate in the expenditure of the vast revenues collected by the general government. Other sections of the Union want a Navy, fortifications, and all the train of improvements, breakwaters, lighthouses, &c. necessary to secure and invigorate the foreign and coasting trade. They ought to have them. The West has cheerfully co-operated in granting them; and he trusted, would continue to do so. But, in their turn, they ought to unite, for their own sakes, as well as for the West, in the establishment of a system which is useful to all, and indispensable to the prosperity of the Western country. He trusted that the West would never in any contingency, pause to calculate the value of this Union. Whatever might be the fate of Internal Improvements, that Union was of inestimable benefit. But it might appeal to the justice, liberality and fraternal feelings of other portions of our common country, to sustain the only system of policy in which it had a direct and immediate interest.

Mr. Clay regretted a late unfavorable indication in respect to this important interest. He could not concur in the reasons assigned for the rejection of the Maysville bill. He could not think of that measure without the deepest surprize [sic], regret and mortification. No State in the Union had more zealously devoted itself to the cause of Internal Improvements than Kentucky. This it had done upon those broad, liberal and national considerations, which had ever guided the conduct of the people of that State in respect to the general government. Scarcely any State in the Union had enjoyed so little direct advantage from the exercises of power by the General Government, as that State. Not one cent of the public treasure of the Union had ever been applied to the erection of any Road or Canal within its limits, expect to that at Louisville, in which other States are much more interested than she is. Under such circumstances, to be selected as the first victim; to have a most important Road lying within that State, though a mere link of a much more extensive chain reaching into other States, singled out for the application of an extra-ordinary power: to be designated as the State, in regard to whose interests the settled practice of the government, during a period of 25 years, must be overturned and set aside—was, to say the least of it, very hard.

The present President, Mr. Clay did not doubt, had, with the most patriotic intentions, when in the Senate of the United States voted for an appropriation to a Canal, of only about 14 miles in extent, in the State of Delaware, uniting the waters of the Delaware and Chesapeake. That Canal was commenced, and has been completed. . . . He presumed that the President gave it his support, because he thought the object was a national one. Mr. C. thought so too, and voted for it. But if it be national, that character cannot be derived from its length, but from the purposes and uses to which, in war as well as in peace, it might be applied. That is the true criterion; and if it be applied to the Maysville Road, Mr. C.

must think that it ought to be considered as a national work, whether regarded by itself, or in connection with contemplated prolongations of it Northwestwardly and Southwestwardly.

See Robert Seager II, ed., *The Papers of Henry Clay*, vol. 8, *Candidate, Compromiser, Whig* (Lexington: University Press of Kentucky, 1984), 238–39.

HENRY CLAY, SPEECH IN CINCINNATI, OHIO, AUGUST 3, 1830

. . . [I]f the road facilitates, in a considerable degree, the transportation of the mail to a considerable portion of the union, and, at the same time, promotes internal commerce among several states, and may tend to accelerate the movement of armies and the distribution of the munitions of war—it is of national consideration. Tested by this, the Maysville road was undoubtedly national.

See Robert Seager II, ed., *The Papers of Henry Clay*, vol. 8, *Candidate, Compromiser, Whig* (Lexington: University Press of Kentucky, 1984), 244.

THE "EATON AFFAIR"

No episode of Jackson's administration quite encapsulated his tendency to view every disagreement as personal and to throw himself headlong into any issue at all about which he felt strongly as the social imbroglio that came to be known as the "Eaton Affair." This escapade also highlighted the growing rift in Jackson's cabinet between Secretary of State Martin Van Buren and his allies on the one hand, and Vice President John C. Calhoun and his allies on the other.

Calhoun had become increasingly jealous of Jackson's friend John Eaton and his prominent position in Jackson's inner circle, and Calhoun viewed him as a distinct barrier to his own advancement toward the presidency. Eaton's marriage to a woman with a questionable past named Peggy O'Neil Timberlake provided the chisel that broke the administration in two. A brash and forward woman, her first husband had been a navy lieutenant named John Timberlake who, it was rumored, had killed himself after attempting to defraud the government. Eaton then began giving her financial advice, and soon they were connected romantically. Amid torrents of gossip already about just how many prominent men were linked to this woman ("eleven dozen" was one number that apparently saw much circulation), Jackson counseled Eaton to go ahead and marry her if he loved her, and ignore any rumor and whisperings. Jackson then appointed Eaton his secretary of war, and the scandal began to spread.

Calhoun's wife, along with many other women in the upper echelon of Washington society, shunned Peggy Eaton at any and all social events. Jackson, on the other hand, immediately and almost reflexively took up for her. Chivalry alone was not responsible for the vehemence with which he took up her cause. He had a sense that behind all the scandal were his political enemies, especially Henry Clay, who were all bound and determined to use the mess to wreck his administration. While there were those who hoped that the scandal would cause some in the administration, namely John Eaton, to fall from favor, such conspiracy-mindedness only served to cloud Jackson's judgment and make him hold the course even more dearly.

Even those who were unquestionably Jackson's friends had doubts about Peggy Eaton's virtue, and although such business would rarely qualify as material for cabinet meetings, Jackson used just such an occasion to defend her virtue and set into those calling it into question. He listened intently to reports that Secretary Eaton himself was clear of any scandalous behavior, but insisted loudly that Mrs. Eaton was just as innocent. "She is as chaste as a virgin," he reportedly bellowed when one in attendance would not extrapolate Peggy's virtue from that of her husband.

Better than any other episode of his presidency, the Eaton Affair illustrates Jackson's ability, even eagerness, to conflate the personal and the political. For him, politics was indeed personal, and opponents were enemies. Moreover, if his position was the right and the virtuous one, that of his opponents, by his reasoning, was devoid of virtue—immoral—and not simply mistaken.

JACKSON TO JOHN COFFEE, DECEMBER 6, 1830

. . . I have just received a long letter from my friend McLemore, upon the subject of my cabinet, and Major and Mrs. Eaton. I fear he has been conversant with only those who profess friendship for me, but who would destroy Eaton however unjustly, to injure me. I intend to answer it the first leisure, friendly and frankly. I love my connections, but if it is believed, that I can ever abandon a friend, and that under circumstances with which my friend Eaton is surrounded, they know nothing of me. "[A] friend in need, is a friend indeed" and I loath the wretch that would abandon his friends, for the smiles of a faction. [B]y me it never has or will be done. Ere long I will have my cabinet as it ought to be, a unit. The double dealing of J.C.C. is perfectly unmasked. [H]e is now as to myself perfectly harmless.

See John Spenser Bassett, ed., *The Correspondence of Andrew Jackson* (Washington, D.C.: Carnegie Institute of Washington, 1929), 4:212.

JACKSON TO JOHN COFFEE, DECEMBER 28, 1830

...I have been much pressed with business, and my domestic concerns have harried my feelings more than any other event of my life. [M]y family were overreached by the hidden intrigues of the great magician [JCC], who believed that the popularity of Eaton would be in the way of his ambition, and be bestowed upon another, therefore that it was necessary to coerce me to abandon him, by which, I must suffer in the public estimation for having appointed him, and that he might wield me to his views, or secretly use it to my destruction. A man who could secretly make the attempt, as he did in the cabinet in 1818, to destroy me, and that under the strongest professions of friendship, is base enough to do anything. [T]he attempt was on my family, believing if they could be enlisted against Major Eaton, my attachment to them, would compel me to yield Eaton to the fabricated slanders, rather than separate from them. I saw the evil, remonstrated and persuaded my family against the snare, but without effect.

See John Spenser Bassett, ed., *The Correspondence of Andrew Jackson* (Washington, D.C.: Carnegie Institute of Washington, 1929), 4:216.

JACKSON TO MRS. ANDREW J. DONELSON,
JANUARY 20, 1831

My dear Emily,
   ...I cannot close without naming my friend major Eaton. [H]e is the true unvarying friend to me.... You cannot then but suppose how much disquietude it has occasioned to me, that harmony did not exist between you, your dear husband, and him, and his family. [M]rs. Eaton, like all others, may have her imprudencies, if she has, let them be so considered and treated as improprieties, but not treated as a lady without virtue, for my dear Emily, I now assure you, that the time is not far distant when the injuries done her in this respect, will be made manifest. The whole will be traced to what I always suspected, a political maneauvre, by disappointed ambition, to coerce major Eaton out of the cabinet, and lessen my standing with the people, so that they would not against urge my re:election....

See John Spenser Bassett, ed., *The Correspondence of Andrew Jackson* (Washington, D.C.: Carnegie Institute of Washington, 1929), 4:226–27.

JOSIAH S. JOHNSTON TO HENRY CLAY, MARCH 14, 1830

. . . The Jackson party has been divided into the friends of Van Buren— Calhoun & the President—& all with different views, Latterly there has been a tendency to take sides with the two leaders, but this is kept quite secret—The parties present a curious spectacle—It appears as if the General & his friends had got into a false position—A Lady [Peggy Eaton] is Undoubtedly the point upon which the momentous affairs of this Country now turns—The General adheres to the Lady through evil report. [H]is faithful Ministers of State & of War & of the P.[ost] office rally under her flag, with their adherents—The Vice President[,] Treasury, Navy & Law Depts. with many of the friends of General Jackson, & all their partizans rally in the opposition—The General Was determin[e]d to have an Eaton Cabinet—but the peculiar state of parties, induced him to spare Branch for a time, as his removal would have been a signal of separation. . . .

See Robert Seager II, ed., *The Papers of Henry Clay*, vol. 8, *Candidate, Compromiser, Whig* (Lexington: University Press of Kentucky, 1984), 181.

HENRY CLAY TO GEORGE WATTERSON, JULY 21, 1829

. . . I rejoice however, my dear Sir, to perceive that you possess a soul which is not to be subdued by the exertion of tyranny. There is happily a returning sense of patriotism, and judgement [*sic*], already manifest throughout the Union; and I hope both you and I shall live to see the Nation rid of its present misrule, and the Jacksons and the Greens and the Eatons and the host of kindred spirits driven back to their original stations and insignificance. If such men and such measures are to be sanctioned and continued, our hopes of free institutions, with their concomitant blessings would be forever destroyed.

See Robert Seager II, ed., *The Papers of Henry Clay*, vol. 8, *Candidate, Compromiser, Whig* (Lexington: University Press of Kentucky, 1984), 79.

RECOMMENDED READINGS

Cole, Donald B. *The Presidency of Andrew Jackson*. Lawrence: University Press of Kansas, 1993.

Freehling, William W. *Prelude to Civil War: The Nullification Controversy in South Carolina, 1816–1836*. New York: Harper & Row, 1966.

Remini, Robert V. *Andrew Jackson and the Bank War*. New York: W. W. Norton & Co., 1967.

———. *The Life of Andrew Jackson*. New York: Harper & Row, 1988.

Schlesinger, Arthur M., Jr. *The Age of Jackson*. Boston: Little, Brown & Co., 1953.

Sellers, Charles. *The Market Revolution: Jacksonian America, 1815–1846*. New York: Oxford University Press, 1991.

3

MARTIN VAN BUREN

(1837–1841)

Martin Van Buren was the first president to be born in an independent United States and the first to hail from New York. He was also the first president of predominantly Dutch ancestry. His was a humble farming background in the Hudson River valley. Choosing not to follow in his father's occupation (that of a tavern-keeper as well as a farmer), the younger Van Buren began to study and practice law and rapidly became known for his skill and effectiveness. He was eventually drawn into New York politics where he continued to shine. His obvious skill and exceedingly smooth demeanor, coupled with his reddish hair, gained him the nickname the "Red Fox." Van Buren was at the core of a group of younger New York politicians known as the "Albany Regency," who worked to replace the older generation of figures who had controlled the state government for decades. As much as he had a knack for a career as a lawyer, he was even more skillful at the give-and-take and deal-making of party politics. His knack for getting what seemed politically impossible accomplished quickly engendered another nickname—the "Little Magician."

The New York legislature chose him to be a U.S. senator in 1821, and in the wake of the cacophonous presidential election of 1824, Van Buren became a solid supporter of Andrew Jackson, the general's most important one in the North. After a few years in the Senate, he went back to New York to serve as governor, and worked diligently to help in Jackson's 1828 campaign. Traveling far and wide, both in New York State and outside of it, he was able to shape and then hold together the emerging pro-Jackson coalition. In so doing, Van Buren gradually became one of Jackson's closest confidants. He was such a key part of the Jackson organization, the new president rewarded him with the high-profile post of secretary of state. In the coming years, as Jackson and John C. Calhoun, his vice president, fell out over elemental political questions, Van Buren's star rose and he found himself at the head of a faction within the cabinet opposing Calhoun and his supporters. Hoping to distance himself from the various scandals and animosities that were beginning to affect the administration—and in so doing protect his own political future—with the president's agreement he resigned from his post and was nominated by Jackson to be the new minister to Great Britain. From the other side of the Atlantic, he thought, he could further his career while making fewer enemies.

A sound idea, perhaps, but it did not work. He already had plenty of enemies and rivals. Enough of them, in fact, that they were able to block his nomination. It infuriated Jackson, not to say Van Buren himself, but it did not derail his career. Immediately Jackson made it known that the Little Magician would be his choice for vice president in a second Jackson term, for it was clear that for a host of reasons Calhoun would not be continuing in that role. In large part because of Jackson's popularity, Van Buren secured the Democratic nomination for president in 1836. In 1837, he was sworn in as the eighth president of the United States.

Van Buren, for all his charm and affability, was a consummate politician. He often hid his real and tightly held opinions behind a mask of noncommittal remarks. Aside from the enemies he acquired during the Jackson administration, most of whom were frankly hostile toward him only because he was an ally of Jackson, he did not make bitter enemies himself. To the contrary, even rivals like Henry Clay found it difficult to dislike him personally. Although he had been drawn into the bitter quarrels between the Jackson administration and Congress, and into the intrigue and rivalries with the administration itself, Van Buren never drew upon himself the personal opprobrium that someone like Calhoun or Jackson himself did. Nevertheless, he was far from a passive spectator in all the backdoor dealings and scheming that went on.

Such dealings and scheming were formative elements in shaping a new national party system, mastered first by Jackson's supporters, who quickly became known as the Democratic Party. The party in opposition to the Democrats took the label "Whigs," so named because Jackson had been often called "King Andrew I" by his detractors, and in British politics, the opposition to the King manifested itself in a group called Whigs. In fact, however, this American version of the Whig Party was little more than semi-organized opposition to Jackson, much of it intensely and solely personal.

By the time Jackson left office and Van Buren came in, there were two main factions to the Whig Party. On one hand were the national Republicans, personified by Henry Clay and his "American System" and heir to the Hamiltonian idea of an activist national government. Those who worked hard for a national bank, for instance, fell into this camp. On the other hand were the states'-rights professing, wealthy slaveholding Whigs of the South who identified themselves as such primarily because of their hatred of Andrew Jackson and his action during the nullification crisis. Given that many northern Whigs were ardent abolitionists, the Whigs were at best an odd patchwork of opportunists. Eventually, the sectional strains would come to the surface and tear the party apart, but not yet. Their tactic in trying to win the presidency in 1836, by running several different Whig candidates with ties to different sections and hoping to throw the election into the House of Representatives, indicated that they were aware of their schizophrenic nature, but it gained them nothing in the end as the party lost to Jackson's political heir Martin Van Buren.

As president, Van Buren had a full plate of troublesome issues from the very beginning on which he had to take a stand. He inherited a troubled economy made much worse by the economic panic of 1837. President Jackson's financial plan of destroying the Bank of the United States and redistributing the government's money to smaller regional banks had caused a whirlwind of speculation and inflation that then came crashing down when he ordered that the government would only accept payment for debt in specie, not paper money. Far and wide the result had been a crippling economic depression.

To prevent a similar monetary and financial crisis in the future but at the same time to ensure a way to safeguard the government funds, Van Buren proposed what came to be known as the "independent treasury," a way of storing money that was neither national bank nor state bank, but was, quite literally, independent of all ties to government. To counter the economic depression, Van Buren similarly thought that the government should do less rather than more and he readily suggested as much. Inaction, though, was not the course many people expected the government to take. Such ideas made Van Buren seem callous and uncaring, and damaged his reputation in the public eye.

In Congress, fights continued over the big issues of the day, and it was quickly shaping up that no domestic issue was bigger than slavery. Even questions that appeared as though they had little to do with the topic somehow found a way to draw it in. Despite the growing desire to eradicate or at least limit slavery, southern politicians were able to use parliamentary rules to table any and all petitions and legislation regarding slavery. This "gag rule," as it came to be called, enraged northerners who saw it as an encroachment on freedom of speech in Congress, and perfectly indicative of the bitter lengths to which southerners would go to prevent talk of slavery.

Outside of Congress, however, there was no such thing as a "gag rule" on the topic. The broad religious revivals that were sweeping the nation in the 1830s and would soon be labeled the "Second Great Awakening" were converting thousands to the cause of anti-slavery. It became a moral and religious issue like never before. Abolitionists, as they were called, bombarded Congress with petitions and letters, demanding that the government do something about this grievous evil in the very fabric of the country. Some radicals spoke of disunion. Most did not go that far, but nevertheless demanded that the government do something. A little step, a symbolic step of some sort, could at least put the nation on the road to abolition, they hoped. Southerners feared any such little step for the same reason.

Two of Van Buren's other political challenges emerged from foreign affairs involving close neighbors of the United States. To the south, the Republic of Texas, a former province of Mexico that had fought a revolution against that country in 1836 and wound up independent, found itself in the middle of the U.S. debate over territorial expansion. Many in both governments wanted Texas to enter the union as a new state, but while expansion as an idea had adherents, Texas found itself caught up in the middle of the newly interpreted slavery question in the United States. Slavery was now tied to annexation, and whatever position Van Buren took would be controversial somewhere.

The other source of foreign agitation was the revolution fizzling along in Canada in 1837 and the ongoing possibility of sympathetic Americans getting involved. Unresolved border issues formed a background of mutual suspicion but a turn of events in December of that year brought matters to a boil. When it came to be known to Canadian authorities that some New Yorkers were providing arms to the rebels, an expedition crossed the Niagara River into New York and destroyed the ship that was being used. One American was killed in the ensuing melee, and it all threatened to blow up into a major problem between the United States and Great Britain. Determined that it would not, Van Buren nevertheless had a tricky course to plot.

Given all he had to deal with, and the wide array of challenges, so many of which could have easily turned into a serious crisis, Van Buren's four years as president were remarkably stable. No single problem spun out of control. It is likely that Van Buren himself deserves a good deal of the credit for this. The course of action he routinely chose to follow was consistently that which caused the least amount of trouble. Perhaps detractors could charge that this merely deferred trouble for another day, and realistically, such a charge is not wholly wrong. But it does not lessen the significance of the stability Van Buren was able to nurture, especially after eight years of the political tumult of the Jackson administration.

Van Buren was never the successor to Jackson that many Jacksonians hoped for, though. What really gave him the most trouble was that he was simply not Andrew Jackson. Jackson had dominated the political scene for years, and Van Buren did not have the appeal that Jackson did. His moderation and drab personality (compared with Jackson, of course) eroded what was weak popularity and made him vulnerable to Whig rivals as the election of 1840 approached. When the Whigs nominated their own war hero, General William Henry Harrison, to bear their standard instead of the more controversial but anticipated Henry Clay, Van Buren was doomed. He lost the election by a wide electoral margin. He would later return to presidential politics in 1848 as the "Free Soil" candidate, but never achieved the success he had known earlier in his career. He died in 1862.

THE ECONOMIC PANIC OF 1837

Martin Van Buren opposed any policy that resulted in the gathering together in the national government of various powers not expressly delegated to it by the Constitution. He was, simply, a states' rights man, even though most of the other politicians who avidly followed this position were southerners. The Panic of 1837 and the economic depression that came along with it provided a distinct challenge to his political philosophy. As he rose in his career, Van Buren had never been faced with any problem quite so profound as this one. Furthermore, despite the key roles he played in the Jackson administration, he was never much in the public eye and consequently never felt the pressures to which Jackson had responded so adeptly and effectively. But now Van Buren was president, and was therefore the target of demands from all around the country that he do something to alleviate the economic distress. In this first test of the Van Buren administration, the memory of Andrew Jackson still hung heavy in the Washington air. Jackson had proven to be the friend of the common man when he declared war on, and destroyed, the Bank of the United States, and by and large his stated policy was to give the people what they wanted. It was to be expected, perhaps, that his successor would be equally as responsive to the cries of the people.

The new president, however, was not Jackson, and the response he gave in his Special Session message just a few months after taking office served notice of this fact most clearly. What he said was the last thing most people expected him to say, and ranks as one of the great scoldings ever administered by any president to the American people. His states' rights ideas were made manifest by his determination that the national government would not be getting involved in the crisis because to do so, despite the severity of the depression, would be to overstep its constitutional bounds. Jackson had never told the people that they expected too much from their government, even when he had vetoed internal improvement bills. Van Buren, however, took that position clearly.

Henry Clay, for one, had clearly expected that the president would take some kind of action, saying that it would be "treachery" to do nothing.

He therefore was surprised and disappointed at the president's position. He was not the only one.

FROM VAN BUREN'S *SPECIAL SESSION MESSAGE*, SEPTEMBER 4, 1837

. . . Those who look to the action of this Government for specific aid to the citizen to relieve embarrassments arising from losses by revulsions in commerce and credit lose sight of the ends for which it was created and the powers with which it is clothed. It was established to give security to us all in our lawful and honorable pursuits, under the lasting safeguard of republican institutions. It was not intended to confer special favors on individuals or on any classes of them, to create systems of agriculture, manufactures, or trade, or to engage in them either separately or in connection with individual citizens or organized associations. If its operations were to be directed for the benefit of any one class, equivalent favors must in justice be extended to the rest, and the attempt to bestow such favors with an equal hand, or even to select those who should most deserve them, would never be successful.

All communities are apt to look to government for too much. Even in our own country, where its powers and duties are so strictly limited, we are prone to do so, especially at periods of sudden embarrassment and distress. But this ought not to be. The framers of our excellent Constitution and the people who approved it with calm and sagacious deliberation acted at the time on a sounder principle. They wisely judged that the less government interferes with private pursuits the better for the general prosperity. It is not its legitimate object to make men rich or to repair by direct grants of money or legislation in favor of particular pursuits losses not incurred in the public service. This would be substantially to use the property of some for the benefit of others. But its real duty—that duty the performance of which makes a good government the most precious of human blessings—is to enact and enforce a system of general laws commensurate with, but not exceeding, the objects of its establishment, and to leave every citizen and every interest to reap under its benign protection the rewards of virtue, industry, and prudence.

. . . If, therefore, I refrain from suggesting to Congress any specific plan for regulating the exchanges of the country, relieving mercantile embarrassments, or interfering with the ordinary operations of foreign or domestic commerce, it is from a conviction that such measures are not within the constitutional province of the General Government, and that their adoption would not promote the real and permanent welfare of those they might be designed to aid.

The difficulties and distresses of the times, though unquestionably great, are limited in their extent, and can not be regarded as affecting the permanent prosperity of the nation.

See *Messages and Papers of the Presidents* (New York: Bureau of National Literature, 1897), 4:1541–63.

Against the Van Buren Economic Policy

HENRY CLAY TO MATTHEW L. DAVIS, JULY 3, 1837

. . . We are here still in the dark as to the purposes of the Admon in regard to measures for correcting the disorders of the Currency and Exchanges. My latest information from Washington is that they are not for a National bank, nor a treasury bank, but that their inclination is to cut all connexion with all banks and to collect and disburse the public revenue in specie only. I think finally they must abandon that scheme. It would be a most singular spectacle to behold a hard-money Government and a paper money people. It would be base treachery on the part of the Government to lead the people into the mire and then to leave them sticking there. . . . I expected that the Admon would promulgate some plan of relief prior to the approaching Elections. Their partizans are in great confusion for the want of a cue. It is perhaps better for us that they should remain in the dark.

See Robert Seager II, ed., *The Papers of Henry Clay*, vol. 9, *The Whig Leader* (Lexington: University Press of Kentucky, 1984), 55.

HENRY CLAY TO HENRY CLAY JR., SEPTEMBER 8, 1837

The Message (of which I send you a Copy) has disappointed everybody, and leaves the Country nothing to expect for its relief from Congress. Such is the general apprehension. We shall see in future developements [*sic*] if any thing good can be done.

See Robert Seager II, ed., *The Papers of Henry Clay*, vol. 9, *The Whig Leader* (Lexington: University Press of Kentucky, 1984), 73.

SLAVERY AND ABOLITIONISTS

Throughout the 1830s, the abolitionist movement began to grow significantly. As it grew, it redefined its tactics and its goal from that of endorsing a program of gradual emancipation to that of immediate abolition. The notion that American slaves could be gradually emancipated had been circulating around the government for decades. Many of the founders had even embraced such ideas, although George Washington had been the only one to actually put provisions to free his slaves into his will. Thomas Jefferson and others had worried about slavery and its effect on national unity, but had always worried about the latter more than the former. Consequently, nothing was done. Year in and year out, there was talk, but no action. Slowly, this inaction made those opposed to slavery realize that the national government was simply unwilling to face the issue directly.

By the 1830s, anti-slavery societies were springing up across New England and southward into New York. The beginning of abolitionist newspapers, especially William Lloyd Garrison's Boston-based *The Liberator*, helped spread the word of abolition and fanned passions on both sides of the question. At first, Garrison and abolitionists like him hoped to win over the hearts of slaveholders, showing them the evil of their actions, with the idea that they would then embrace abolition willingly. In this way, slavery would pass away quietly and the dictates of conscience, both north and south, would triumph.

It did not take long before many in the movement soured on this tactic of gentle persuasion. Over the course of the 1830s, abolitionists split into radical and moderate camps, with Garrison casting his lot with the radicals. He denounced the Constitution as "an agreement with hell," and believed that fundamental, sweeping reform of society was the only way to purge the evil of slavery. Others said that abolition was necessary even if the price was complete disunion. Many in the North felt the sin of slavery would condemn the entire country, even though it was localized in the South. Such activists believed that no one in the North could be innocent of complicity in the sin, therefore, if he refused to speak out and take action.

One of the key goals of the abolitionist movement was to ban slavery in Washington, D.C. They believed that legal slavery in the American capital was among the most grievous and hypocritical offenses to humanity, given that the Declaration of Independence was usually on public display somewhere in the city and, it was assumed, formed the basis of the nation's philosophy. Congress had express control over the politics and policy in the Federal City, as it was usually called, so the bugbear of states' rights would have no influence. Without question, Congress could do what it wanted without stepping onto any other institution's ground.

The existence of slavery in Washington, however, was just as symbolic to the pro-slavery faction as it was to the abolitionists. As the abolitionist movement grew louder, slaveholders grew more restless. Everywhere they looked in the North they saw a movement whose strength they began to regularly overestimate. They became more defensive and determined to preserve their "peculiar institution" as it was called. Behind much of their unease lay the fear of violent slave insurrection, a likelihood, they thought, if such heated rhetoric and radical plans drifted southward.

For the president, his supreme worry was the discord and animosity this situation was quickly creating. No president wanted to preside over the implosion of the union over the cause of slavery. Van Buren adopted as his position a "do nothing" stance, believing that this is what the founders had done, thereby preserving the union of states. Doing nothing, however, was no longer a way to quiet the abolitionists. Doing nothing had gone on quite long enough for them. Organized opposition to slavery had already adopted a firm goal in opposition to Van Buren's course of inaction.

FROM VAN BUREN'S *INAUGURAL ADDRESS*, MARCH 1837

. . . The last, perhaps the greatest, of the prominent sources of discord and disaster supposed to lurk in our political condition was the institution of domestic slavery. Our forefathers were deeply impressed with the delicacy of this subject, and they treated it with a forbearance so evidently wise that in spite of every sinister foreboding it never until the present period disturbed the tranquillity of our common country. Such a result is sufficient evidence of the justice and the patriotism of their course; it is evidence not to be mistaken that an adherence to it can prevent all embarrassment from this as well as from every other anticipated cause of difficulty or danger. Have not recent events made it obvious to the slightest reflection that the least deviation from this spirit of forbearance is injurious to every interest, that of humanity included? Amidst the violence of excited passions this generous and fraternal feeling has been sometimes disregarded; and standing as I now do before my countrymen, in this high place of honor and of trust, I can not refrain from anxiously invoking my fellow-citizens never to be deaf to its dictates. Perceiving before my election the deep interest this subject was beginning to excite, I believed it a solemn duty fully to make known my sentiments in regard to it. . . . I then declared that if the desire of those of my countrymen who were favorable to my election was gratified "I must go into the Presidential chair the inflexible and uncompromising opponent of every attempt on the part of Congress to abolish slavery in the District of Columbia against the wishes of the slaveholding States, and also with a determination equally decided to resist the slightest interference with it in the States where it exists." . . . It now only remains to add that no bill conflicting with these views can ever receive my constitutional sanction.

These opinions have been adopted in the firm belief that they are in accordance with the spirit that actuated the venerated fathers of the Republic, and that succeeding experience has proved them to be humane, patriotic, expedient, honorable, and just.

... Here and there, indeed, scenes of dangerous excitement have occurred, terrifying instances of local violence have been witnessed, and a reckless disregard of the consequences of their conduct has exposed individuals to popular indignation; but neither masses of the people nor sections of the country have been swerved from their devotion to the bond of union and the principles it has made sacred. It will be ever thus.

See *Messages and Papers of the Presidents* (New York: Bureau of National Literature, 1897), 4:1530–37.

Against Van Buren's Position

THE CONSTITUTION OF THE AMERICAN ANTI-SLAVERY SOCIETY, ADOPTED DECEMBER 4, 1833

Whereas the Most High God "hath made of one blood all nations of men to dwell on all the face of the earth," and hath commanded them to love their neighbors as themselves; and whereas, our National Existence is based upon this principle, as recognized in the Declaration of Independence, "that all mankind are created equal, and that they are endowed by their Creator with certain inalienable rights, among which are life, liberty, and the pursuit of happiness" ... and whereas, we believe that it is practicable, by appeals to the consciences, hearts, and interests of the people, to awaken a public sentiment throughout the nation that will be opposed to the continuance of Slavery in any part of the Republic, and by effecting the speedy abolition of Slavery, prevent a general convulsion; and whereas, we believe we owe it to the oppressed, to our fellow-citizens who hold slaves, to our whole country, to posterity, and to God, to do all that is lawfully in our power to bring about the extinction of Slavery, we do hereby agree, with a prayerful reliance on the Divine aid, to form ourselves into a society, to be governed by the following Constitution:

ARTICLE II.—The objects of this Society are the entire abolition of Slavery in the United States. While it admits that each State, in which Slavery exists, has, by the Constitution of the United States, the exclusive right to *legislate* in regard to its abolition in said State, it shall aim to convince all our fellow-citizens, by arguments addressed to their understandings and consciences, that Slaveholding is a heinous crime in the sight of God, and that the duty, safety, and best interests of all concerned, require its *immediate abandonment*, without expatriation. The Society will also endeavor, in a constitutional way, to influence Congress to put an end to the domestic Slave trade, and to abolish Slavery in all those portions of our common country which come under its control, especially in the District of Columbia,—and likewise to prevent the extension of it to any State that may be hereafter admitted to the Union.

See http://douglassarchives.org/aass_a58.htm.

THE UNITED STATES, GREAT BRITAIN, AND CANADA

During Martin Van Buren's administration, there was considerable unrest in Canada along the border with the United States. Rebels fighting against British control of Canada found natural allies just across the border in the United States and it was only a matter of time before ardent, passionate Americans became directly involved. New Yorkers did so by supplying weapons to the rebels. Central to their activity was a good-sized steamship called the *Caroline*, owned by an American. By the autumn of 1837, the *Caroline* was regularly ferrying guns and other supplies from New York out to the Canadian-controlled Navy Island halfway across the river.

British authorities were determined to put an end to this and planned a raid to capture or destroy the *Caroline* while she was docked at the island. When they put their plan in motion, however, and approached Navy Island from the Canadian shore, they discovered that their timing was off, and the *Caroline* was docked on the New York shore instead of on the island. They nevertheless continued across the river, boarded the ship, and after an exchange of gunfire in which one American was killed, set her afire and then adrift out into the river, where she eventually went cascading over Niagara Falls.

Passions in New York exploded. Newspapers were outraged over this invasion and demanded action. President Van Buren was shocked and immediately concerned that the whole affair could easily escalate into a serious international incident and even war. Word coming from New York gave him little reassurance that Americans there would be restrained in their actions, especially if the governor called out the state militia. The British government was steadfast in defending its actions and called the crew of the *Caroline* lawless pirates against whom they had every right to take action, even if it meant pursuing them into the United States.

The questions involved in the affair were complicated ones of nation sovereignty, self-defense, and the sanctity of borders. While condemning the actions of the gunrunners and demanding that American citizens respect the neutrality of the United States in whatever rebellion was going on in Canada, Van Buren nonetheless took a hard line against any incursions into American territory. He asked Congress for the authority to prevent Americans from violating neutrality, but also sent a detachment of soldiers to the border under the command of General Winfield Scott, with clear orders to prevent any other such incursions by the British. Through diplomatic channels, he demanded redress.

The excerpts reprinted here give a good account of the unfolding pressure that Van Buren had to face along the border of New York State and Canada. The interplay between Van Buren's secretary of state and British official Henry Fox shows the president's solid position, as do his periodic updates to Congress on how the situation was playing out.

H. W. ROGERS TO VAN BUREN, DECEMBER 30, 1837

. . . Our whole frontier is in commotion, and I fear it will be difficult to restrain our citizens from avenging by a resort to arms this flagrant invasion of our territory. Everything that can be done will be by the public authorities to prevent so injudicious a movement. The respective sheriffs of Erie and Niagara have taken the responsibility of calling out the militia to guard the frontier and prevent any further depredations.

See *Messages and Papers of the Presidents* (New York: Bureau of National Literature, 1897), 4:1618.

VAN BUREN TO CONGRESS, JANUARY 5, 1838

. . . Recent experience on the southern boundary of the United States and the events now daily occurring on our northern frontier have abundantly shown that the existing laws are insufficient to guard against hostile invasion from the United States of the territory of friendly and neighboring nations.

The laws in force provide sufficient penalties for the punishment of such offenses after they have been committed, and provided the parties can be found, but the Executive is powerless in many cases to prevent the commission of them, even when in possession of ample evidence of an intention on the part of evil-disposed persons to violate our laws.

Your attention is called to this defect in our legislation. It is apparent that the Executive ought to be clothed with adequate power effectually to restrain all persons within our jurisdiction from the commission of acts of this character. They tend to disturb the peace of the country and inevitably involve the Government in perplexing controversies with foreign powers. I recommend a careful revision of all the laws now in force and such additional enactments as may be necessary to vest in the Executive full power to prevent injuries being inflicted upon neighboring nations by the unauthorized and unlawful acts of citizens of the United States or of other persons who may be within our jurisdiction and subject to our control.

See *Messages and Papers of the Presidents* (New York: Bureau of National Literature, 1897), 4:1616.

VAN BUREN TO CONGRESS, JANUARY 8, 1838

. . . In the highly excited state of feeling on the northern frontier, occasioned by the disturbances in Canada, it was to be apprehended that causes of complaint might arise on the line dividing the United States from Her Britannic Majesty's dominions. Every precaution was therefore taken on our part authorized by the existing laws, and as the troops of the Provinces were embodied on the Canadian side it was hoped that no serious violation of the rights of the United States would be permitted to occur. I regret, however, to inform you that an outrage of a most aggravated character has been committed, accompanied by a hostile though temporary invasion of our territory, producing the strongest feelings of resentment on the part of our citizens in the neighborhood and on the whole border line, and that the excitement previously existing has been alarmingly increased. To guard against the possible recurrence of any similar act I have thought it indispensable to call out a portion of the militia, to be posted on that frontier. The documents herewith presented to Congress show the character of the outrage committed, the measures taken in consequence of its occurrence, and the necessity for resorting to them.

See *Messages and Papers of the Presidents* (New York: Bureau of National Literature, 1897), 4:1618.

SECRETARY OF STATE JOHN FORSYTH TO BRITISH AMBASSADOR HENRY S. FOX, JANUARY 5, 1838

. . . By the direction of the President of the United States, I have the honor to communicate to you a copy of the evidence furnished to this Department of an extraordinary outrage committed from Her Britannic Majesty's Province of Upper Canada on the persons and property of citizens of the United States within the jurisdiction of the State of New York.

The destruction of the property and the assassination of citizens of the United States on the soil of New York at the moment when, as is well known to you, the President was anxiously endeavoring to allay the excitement and earnestly seeking to prevent any unfortunate occurrence on the frontier of Canada have produced upon his mind the most painful emotions of surprise and regret. It will necessarily form the subject of a demand for redress upon Her Majesty's Government. . . . Not doubting the disposition of the government of Upper Canada to do its duty in punishing the aggressors and preventing future outrage, the President nevertheless has deemed it necessary to order a sufficient force on the frontier to repel any attempt of a like character and to make known to you that if it should occur he can not be answerable for the effects of the indignation of the neighboring people of the United States.

See *Messages and Papers of the Presidents* (New York: Bureau of National Literature, 1897), 4:1621.

HENRY S. FOX TO JOHN FORSYTH, FEBRUARY 6, 1838

. . . With reference to the letters which, by direction of the President, you addressed to me on the 5th and 19th ultimo, respecting the capture and destruction of the steamboat Caroline by a Canadian force on the American side of the Niagara River, within the jurisdiction of the State of New York, I have now the honor to communicate to you the copy of a letter upon that subject which I have received from Sir Francis Head, lieutenant-governor of the Province of Upper Canada, with divers reports and depositions annexed.

The piratical character of the steamboat *Caroline* and the necessity of self-defense and self-preservation under which Her Majesty's subjects acted in destroying that vessel would seem to be sufficiently established.

At the time when the event happened the ordinary laws of the United States were not enforced within the frontier district of the State of New York. The authority of the law was overborne publicly by piratical violence. Through such violence Her Majesty's subjects in Upper Canada had already severely suffered, and they were threatened with still further injury and outrage. This extraordinary state of things appears naturally and necessarily to have impelled them to consult their own security by pursuing and destroying the vessel of their piratical enemy wheresoever they might find her.

See *Messages and Papers of the Presidents* (New York: Bureau of National Literature, 1897), 4:1677–78.

FROM VAN BUREN'S *SECOND ANNUAL MESSAGE TO CONGRESS*, DECEMBER 3, 1838

... I had hoped that the respect for the laws and regard for the peace and honor of their own country which have ever characterized the citizens of the United States would have prevented any portion of them from using any means to promote insurrection in the territory of a power with which we are at peace, and with which the United States are desirous of maintaining the most friendly relations. I regret deeply, however, to be obliged to inform you that this has not been the case. Information has been given to me, derived from official and other sources, that many citizens of the United States have associated together to make hostile incursions from our territory into Canada and to aid and abet insurrection there, in violation of the obligations and laws of the United States and in open disregard of their own duties as citizens. This information has been in part confirmed by a hostile invasion actually made by citizens of the United States, in conjunction with Canadians and others, and accompanied by a forcible seizure of the property of our citizens and an application thereof to the prosecution of military operations against the authorities and people of Canada.

The results of these criminal assaults upon the peace and order of a neighboring country have been, as was to be expected, fatally destructive to the misguided or deluded persons engaged in them and highly injurious to those in whose behalf they are professed to have been undertaken. ... If an insurrection existed in Canada, the amicable dispositions of the United States toward Great Britain, as well as their duty to themselves, would lead them to maintain a strict neutrality and to restrain their citizens from all violations of the laws which have been passed for its enforcement. But this Government recognizes a still higher obligation to repress all attempts on the part of its citizens to disturb the peace of a country where order prevails or has been reestablished. Depredations by our citizens upon nations at peace with the United States, or combinations for committing them, have at all times been regarded by the American Government and people with the greatest abhorrence. Military incursions by our citizens into countries so situated, and the commission of acts of violence on the members thereof, in order to effect a change- in their government, or under any pretext whatever, have from the commencement of our Government been held equally criminal on the part of those engaged in them, and as much deserving of punishment as would be the disturbance of the public peace by the perpetration of similar acts within our own territory.

... [W]hether the interest or the honor of the United States requires that they should be made a party to any such struggle, and by inevitable consequence to the war which is waged in its support, is a question which by our Constitution is wisely left to Congress alone to decide. . . . I can not but hope that the good sense and patriotism, the regard for the honor and reputation of their country, the respect for the laws which they have themselves enacted for their own government, and the love of order for which the mass of our people have been so long and so justly distinguished will deter the comparatively few who are engaged in them from a further prosecution of such desperate enterprises.

See *Messages and Papers of the Presidents* (New York: Bureau of National Literature, 1897), 4:1700–1721.

THE "INDEPENDENT TREASURY" PLAN

In the wake of Andrew Jackson's administration, during which government funds were withdrawn from the Bank of the United States, a Bank extension bill was vetoed, and the Bank's charter allowed to expire, the Van Buren administration had to design a new method by which to manage the nation's funds. Van Buren had made it clear that he would not support a renewed Bank of the United States. On the contrary, he supported the idea that government funds should be removed as completely as possible from both the Executive Branch and from any sort of private enterprise. The idea taking shape, which he spelled out early in his term, became known as the "Independent Treasury" plan. The Independent Treasury would be a simple storehouse for the money the government took in via taxes, tariffs, and any other revenue-producing activity. The independence of the plan would guard against corruption or unfair advantages accruing to any part of society that had easier access to loans or "inside information" than the rest of society. In Van Buren's plan, the government's money would simply sit and wait to be used for government needs, and not be used in any stimulative action for the national economy.

In the eyes of the opposition, the Independent Treasury plan would leave the government and the U.S. economy without any sort of mechanism for directing and encouraging economic growth. The economy was bigger and more complicated than ever before, and tied the different regions of the country together more tightly. If a national bank had been needed when Alexander Hamilton had been secretary of the treasury, it was certainly needed even more so now. In addition, other nations had powerful central banks, and Whigs believed that not to have one in the United States would cause a distinct disadvantage for the American economy in competition with British goods, French goods, and even the new trade alliance that was emerging among the many independent German states.

For the president, these concerns were not as important as his own belief that a national bank operated unfairly and benefited one economic sector over others. The only way to ensure fairness, and to honor the constitutional limitations on the national government's power, was to sever the connections between banking and government. On this President Van Buren was determined. He began to outline this plan in his special session message in September 1837, and fleshed it out more in his first annual address to Congress that December. Excerpts from both addresses are provided here in order to more fully understand the background of the plan, Van Buren's concept of why it was needed, what he hoped to achieve by its implementation, and some of the details which the president worked out. There was plenty of bitter opposition to the Independent Treasury plan, and not just from famous Whigs like Henry Clay. Interestingly enough, many who opposed the Independent Treasury plan did so because they believed that its inevitable failure would actually make a return of a powerful national bank more likely. The standard practice of Democrats had been to support state banks, and for them, Van Buren's scheme was no more welcome than Clay's.

FROM VAN BUREN'S *SPECIAL SESSION MESSAGE*, SEPTEMBER 4, 1837

. . . [I]t is apparent that the events of the last few months have greatly augmented the desire, long existing among the people of the United States, to separate the fiscal operations of the Government from those of individuals or corporations.

Again to create a national bank as a fiscal agent would be to disregard the popular will, twice solemnly and unequivocally expressed. On no question of domestic policy is there stronger evidence that the sentiments of a large majority are deliberately fixed, and I can not concur with those who think they see in recent events a proof that these sentiments are, or a reason that they should be, changed.

. . . My own views of the subject are unchanged. They have been repeatedly and unreservedly announced to my fellow-citizens, who with full knowledge of them conferred upon me the two highest offices of the Government. On the last of these occasions I felt it due to the people to apprise them distinctly that in the event of my election I would not be able to cooperate in the reestablishment of a national bank. To these sentiments I have now only to add the expression of an increased conviction that the reestablishment of such a bank in any form, whilst it would not accomplish the beneficial purpose promised by its advocates, would impair the rightful supremacy of the popular will, injure the character and diminish the influence of our political system, and bring once more into existence a concentrated moneyed power, hostile to the spirit and threatening the permanency of our republican institutions.

. . . Surely banks are not more able than the Government to secure the money in their possession against accident, violence, or fraud. The assertion that they are so must assume that a vault in a bank is stronger than a vault in the Treasury, and that directors, cashiers, and clerks not selected by the Government nor under its control are more worthy of confidence than officers selected from the people and responsible to the Government— officers bound by official oaths and bonds for a faithful performance of their duties, and constantly subject to the supervision of Congress.

See *Messages and Papers of the Presidents* (New York: Bureau of National Literature, 1897), 4:1541–63.

FROM VAN BUREN'S *FIRST ANNUAL MESSAGE TO CONGRESS*, DECEMBER 5, 1837

. . . I have found no reason to change my own opinion . . . that there will be neither stability nor safety either in the fiscal affairs of the Government or in the pecuniary transactions of individuals and corporations so long as a connection exists between them which, like the past, offers such strong inducements to make them the subjects of political agitation. Indeed, I am more than ever convinced of the dangers to which the free and unbiased exercise of political opinion—the only sure foundation and safeguard of republican government—would be exposed by any further increase of the already overgrown influence of corporate authorities. I can not, therefore, consistently with my views of duty, advise a renewal of a connection which circumstances have dissolved.

. . . The object of the measure under consideration is to avoid for the future a compulsory connection of this kind. It proposes to place the General Government, in regard to the essential points of the collection, safe-keeping, and transfer of the public money, in a situation which shall relieve it from all dependence on the will of irresponsible individuals or corporations; to withdraw those moneys from the uses of private trade and confide them to agents constitutionally selected and controlled by law; to abstain from improper interference with the industry of the people and withhold inducements to improvident dealings on the part of individuals; to give stability to the concerns of the Treasury; to preserve the measures of the Government from the unavoidable reproaches that flow from such a connection, and the banks themselves from the injurious effects of a supposed participation in the political conflicts of the day, from which they will otherwise find it difficult to escape.

See *Messages and Papers of the Presidents* (New York: Bureau of National Literature, 1897), 4:1590–1612.

Against the Independent Treasury

REPRESENTATIVE WILLIAM B. CALHOUN OF MASSACHUSETTS

. . . If this measure shall receive the sanction of Congress, and pass into the solemn form of a law, the conflict will be but commenced between the system to which the country has been accustomed from the earliest days of the republic, and that system which bears upon its front the baptismal name of "untried experiment."

. . . I cannot join the crusade, which the adoption of this measure, as the settled policy of the Government, cannot but beat up against the long-standing order of things. I will not consent ruthlessly to pull down an ancient institution, until I can be convinced the substitute for it shall better answer the purpose. I am contented, nay, anxious to reform, where reform is necessary; but I cannot yield to what I feel confident must be the effect of this bill, if carried through to its outside purposes. I cannot agree to destroy.

This, then, is the stable and firm ground upon which I plant my opposition to this sub-Treasury scheme. Carried out into all its consequences, the effect of it must be, to change the framework of society; to revolutionize property and business; to reduce the former indefinitely and most essentially, and to withdraw the latter into the hands of the few; . . . to paralyze credit; to deaden the vigorous arm of industry; and, finally, and in one word, to give to wealth that ascendancy which nothing but free competition can break down, and to make poverty hug its chains more closely.

. . . I will not dwell upon the numerous objections which are urged against this bill with great force as a matter of business. Its insecurity forms of itself an abundant reason why it should be distrusted and repudiated. The placing of public funds in the hands of individuals for safekeeping or disbursement, leads the depositary into that temptation from which every prudent man should pray to be delivered.

See *Register of Debates in Congress*, 25th Cong., 1st Sess., vol. xiv, pt. 2, columns 1466–67.

REPRESENTATIVE JAMES M. MASON OF VIRGINIA

. . . No, sir, in my humble judgment the danger of recurrence to a national bank is to be looked for in the very opposite quarter: in the immature conception and hurried execution of this sub-Treasury scheme. . . . [S]uppose they should fail; suppose it should be found impractical to carry out the new scheme; that the currency should grow worse; that bank paper should continue irredeemable; and the people become wearied out with your rigid exaction of coin from them, while nothing but paper is paid to them: I ask you, and I put it to the serious consideration of the country, what remedy would then be found? You could not fall back upon the State banks. They had just been divorced, and common decency would forbid the new espousal. Where, then, would you find refuge? Why, sir, as was done once before, in the arms of a national bank, and nowhere else.

. . . But I can see no advantage, and on the contrary a fruitful source of mischief, in making Government officers the keepers of the cash. Place about them what guards you may, in the shape of commissioners, inspectors, or whatever else, peculation will be endless. There is no security in it, and it will involve heavy and unnecessary expense. The chief and over-ruling objection, however, is the endless source of patronage to which it would give rise. Make the machinery as simple as you may, and open to view, wherever money is, temptation will creep in, and corruption in every form following at its heels. But the money can be safely kept, under the most ample security, and freed from every objection of patronage or political influence, by a simple system of special deposites [sic] in the State banks, remaining always in specie, the separate property of the Government, and paid out in kind upon drafts from the Treasury.

See *Register of Debates in Congress*, 25th Cong., 1st Sess., vol. xiv, pt. 2, columns 1432, 1435.

TEXAS AND THE UNITED STATES

In 1836, the Mexican state of Texas rebelled against the government of Mexican dictator Santa Anna. Santa Anna himself led a large army northward into Texas to crush the rebellion, the first stage of which, to his reckoning, was to obliterate the rebel garrison in San Antonio that was holed up in the old mission known as the Alamo. The battle that ensued captivated the attention of people in the United States and there was much sympathy for the Texian (as "Texans" were then known) cause, especially in the southern United States. Shortly after the fall of the Alamo, Texas declared its independence, and General Sam Houston, an ex-U.S. senator from Tennessee and one of Andrew Jackson's closest political allies and personal friends, led the remaining Texian army eastward before Santa Anna's dogged pursuit. Arrogant and overconfident, Santa Anna encamped his army within sight of Houston's army on the afternoon of April 21, 1836. Houston in turn immediately attacked and routed the

Mexican forces in one of the most one-sided battles in military history. After his capture, Santa Anna was forced to sign a peace treaty and send his army back to Mexico, across the Rio Grande.

Many in Texas wanted to join the United States immediately after gaining independence from Mexico. Others, however, wanted the Republic of Texas to remain independent. Many in the United States, especially in the South, saw the annexation of Texas as a means of bringing at least one new slave state into the union and probably more. Some southerners even regarded Texas as legitimate American territory in the first place, a part of the original Louisiana Purchase deviously given away by then–Secretary of State John Quincy Adams in 1819. Many northerners bitterly opposed annexation—some opposed any contact with Texas at all—because of the certainty that the southern states were looking for any excuse at all to spread slavery. President Martin Van Buren was opposed to annexation—making his position clear through his secretary of state—and no matter how hard its supporters worked, including the minister from Texas to the United States, Memucan Hunt (who boldly threatened economic retaliation if Texas were denied), he held his ground.

SECRETARY OF STATE JOHN FORSYTH TO MEMUCAN HUNT, AUGUST 25, 1837

The question of the *annexation* of a foreign independent State to the United States has never before been presented to this Government. Since the adoption of their constitution, two large additions have been made to the domain originally claimed by the United States. In acquiring them this Government was not actuated by a mere thirst for sway over a broader space. Paramount interests of many members of the confederacy, and the permanent well being of all, imperatively urged upon this Government the necessity of an extension of its jurisdiction over Louisiana and Florida. As peace, however, was our cherished policy . . . we patiently endured for a time serious inconveniences and privations, and sought a transfer of those regions by negotiations and not . . . conquest.

. . . The circumstance, however, of their being colonial possessions of France and Spain, and therefore dependent on the metropolitan Governments, renders those transactions materially different from that which would be presented by the question of the annexation of Texas. The latter is a State with an independent Government, acknowledged as such by the United States. . . . Whether the constitution of the United States contemplated the annexation of such a State, and if so, in what manner that object is to be effected, are questions, in the opinion of the President, it would be inexpedient, under existing circumstances, to agitate.

So long as Texas shall remain at war, while the United States are at peace with her adversary, the proposition of [annexation] . . . necessarily involves the question of war with that adversary. The United States are bound to Mexico by a treaty of amity and commerce, which will be scrupulously observed on their part, so long as it can be reasonably hoped that Mexico will perform her duties and respect our rights under it.

. . . The inducements mentioned by General Hunt, for the United States to annex Texas to their territory, are duly appreciated, but powerful and weighty as certainly they are, they are light when opposed in the scale of reason to treaty obligations and respect for that integrity of character by which the United States have sought to distinguish themselves since the establishment of their right to claim a place in the great family of nations.

See *Message from the President of the United States, in compliance with a resolution of the House of Representatives of the 13th instant, respecting an Annexation of Texas to the United States*, 25th Cong., 1st Sess., October 3, 1837, 12–13.

MEMUCAN HUNT TO JOHN FORSYTH, SEPTEMBER 12, 1837

. . . The honorable Mr. Forsyth will pardon the undersigned for expressing the opinion which appears to him undeniable—that a sovereign Power has as perfect a right to dispose of the whole of itself, and a second Power to acquire it, as it has to dispose of only a part of itself, and second Power to acquire that part only; and that the acquisition of the whole territory of a sovereign Power could no more be objected to on the ground of constitutional right, than the acquisition of a part of that territory only.

. . . Should, however, the foreign commercial and other relations of the republic of Texas necessarily become such as seriously to affect the interests of the United States, or any portion thereof, the undersigned conceives that it would be unreasonable for the Government and people who had been freely proffered all she could bestow and yet declined the offer, to complain of her on the ground of looking to her own interest primarily. Texas has generously offered to merge her national sovereignty in a domestic one, and to become a constituent part of this great confederacy. The refusal of this Government to accept the overture must forever screen her from the imputation of willfully injuring the great interests of the United States, should such a result accrue from any commercial or other relations which she may find it necessary or expedient to enter into with foreign nations.

Should it be found necessary . . . for the proper promotion of the interests of her own citizens, to lay high duties upon the cotton-bagging so extensively manufactured in the Western States, and upon the pork and beef and bread-stuffs, so abundantly produced in that region, such as would amount to an almost total prohibition of the introduction of these articles into the country, much as her Government and people would regret the necessity of the adoption of such a policy, she would be exculpated from the slightest imputation of blame for taking care of her own welfare and prosperity after having been refused admission into this Union.

See *Message from the President of the United States, in compliance with a resolution of the House of Representatives of the 13th instant, respecting an Annexation of Texas to the United States*, 25th Cong., 1st Sess., October 3, 1837, 15–17.

RECOMMENDED READINGS

Mushkat, Jerome, and Joseph G. Rayback. *Martin Van Buren: Law, Politics, and the Shaping of Republican Ideology*. DeKalb: Northern Illinois University Press, 1997.

Niven, John. *Martin Van Buren: The Romantic Age of American Politics*. New York: Oxford University Press, 1983.

Remini, Robert V. *Martin Van Buren and the Making of the Democratic Party*. New York: Columbia University Press, 1959.

Silbey, Joel H. *Martin Van Buren and the Emergence of Popular American Politics*. Lanham, Md.: Rowman and Littlefield, 2002.

Wilson, Major L. *The Presidency of Martin Van Buren*. Lawrence: University Press of Kansas, 1984.

4

WILLIAM HENRY HARRISON
AND JOHN TYLER

(1841 and 1841–1845)

Never before had a president died in office. The country was completely unprepared for it to happen, and was utterly grief-stricken when it did. The popular president had been in office only a few months before he was struck down by pneumonia. The city of Washington was draped in black crepe, and the new president solemnly declared a lengthy period of national mourning.

Making it all the more shocking was the president who had fallen. President William Henry Harrison was a famous hero of Indian wars on the midwestern frontier. Specifically, it had been he who defeated the great Shawnee leader known as "The Prophet" in the Battle of Tippecanoe in 1811, and then, during the War of 1812, had led U.S. forces in the defeat of another famous Shawnee leader, Tecumseh, who had allied himself and his people with the British. Until the emergence of Andrew Jackson as the hero of the Battle of New Orleans in 1815, William Henry Harrison was one of the unmatched heroes of the war.

Although in large part because of this, in the popular mind William Henry Harrison was associated with the Midwest and the frontier; in reality he was from Virginia. The Harrisons were one of the oldest and most well-known families in Old Dominion, and William Henry's father was a signer of the Declaration of Independence. The Harrison family home, Berkley plantation, where William Henry was born in 1773, was one of the grandest of the stately plantations lining the James River below Richmond. George Washington himself had given young William Henry Harrison an army commission, and Harrison had taken part in actions against Indian tribes in what was called the Northwest, but he resigned his commission by the end of the 1790s and entered politics.

By 1801 he had worked his way up to governor of the Indiana territory and as such, negotiated several successful treaties with various tribes that opened up more land to American settlement and was part of the political negotiations that split the Northwest into two territories, Indiana and Ohio. Afterwards, he was again governor of the new Indiana Territory, securing its northwestern borders with still another series of treaties. After the War of 1812, Harrison served brief stints as a representative and then a senator from Ohio. As an administrator he was an able, if undistinguished, individual, but it was his reputation as a warrior—and even more so, an Indian fighter—that made him attractive to many Whig leaders as the presidential election of 1836 drew near. They saw Harrison as nothing less than a Whig version of Andrew Jackson, and their answer to Jackson's broad, simplistic, and, in a sense, transpolitical appeal. He was narrowly defeated by Jackson's heir apparent in 1836, due more to the chaotic nature of the national Whig organization and the fact that there were three other high-profile Whigs running nationally than to anything he himself did or did not do.

Because Jackson had been able to capitalize on his military renown and draw voters to him without having to take a firm position on any controversial issue at all, the Whigs determined to unite and do the same. Instead of backing Henry Clay, the longtime champion of such controversial issues such as the bank and internal improvements and the man most identified with the Whig Party, party leaders renominated Harrison in 1840.

The election of 1840 was remarkable as an election of manufactured image. It came to be known as the "Log Cabin and Cider" campaign, because of the Democrats' ill-advised attempt to portray the general as a simplistic frontiersman, with the implication that national politics was far beyond his limited capabilities and understanding. Having championed Jackson for two terms, the Democrats quite simply should have known better. Harrison and the Whigs seized the slogan and made it theirs—a badge of honor representative of the common man, in contrast to the aristocratic Martin Van Buren. Suddenly, Harrison lived in a log cabin and farmed his own plot of land, in addition to drinking hard cider. By downplaying any controversial issues and focusing on this kind of manufactured image (although it was little different from the manufacturing of Jackson's image by the Democrats), Harrison won by a large electoral vote margin, giving the Whig Party its first presidential victory. His time in office, however, was to be the shortest of any president in history.

For all the sadness and sorrow over the loss of the national leader, there was the awareness that the country was faced with a situation it had never faced before. To make the situation more uncertain, compared with General William Henry Harrison, not many people knew much about his vice president, John Tyler of Virginia. How events would play out was anyone's guess.

Like William Henry Harrison, John Tyler also had his roots at a plantation along the James River in Virginia, but was almost twenty years younger than the General. Also in contrast to Harrison, Tyler's career seemed tailor-made for the presidency. After attending the College of William and Mary in Williamsburg, Tyler practiced law and entered politics. He served in the Virginia House of Delegates, the U.S. House of Representatives, as the governor of Virginia, and in the U.S. Senate. While in the Senate, he began drifting away from the Jacksonians in the wake of the nullification crisis and, more generally, due to other instances of Jackson's increasing the power of the presidency at the expense, so he thought, of states. Tyler was eventually one of those who abandoned the Jacksonian Democrats entirely and joined the southern wing of the Whig Party—an organization that had, at least in the South, antipathy toward Jackson as its only unifying factor. As a states' rights man, Tyler had little in common philosophically with his fellow Whigs such as Webster and Clay, but his move caused Democrats in the Virginia legislature to demand his resignation from the Senate.

Four years later, however, Tyler found himself on a presidential ticket. Whigs hoped that a southerner with known states' rights ideas would balance out the nationalism of General Harrison. "Tippecanoe and Tyler, too!" became the memorable campaign slogan and the pair won the election.

After Harrison's death, problems began between the new president and the Whigs who had put him on the ticket. Whigs in Congress like Henry Clay assumed that Tyler would be pliable, to put it mildly, and assent to their programs. Nationalistic Whig legislation began to come out of Congress, but Tyler, who had long been a personal friend of Henry Clay, still retained his states' rights core beliefs. Whigs, apparently, had misjudged Tyler's character. He had abandoned none of his principles when he had joined the presidential ticket, nor had he substantively changed his mind about policies when other Democrats drubbed him out of their party. He vetoed legislation like the Bank of the United States, and soon the Whigs had turned against him. Before long, there was intermittent Whig talk of impeachment. He was a man—and more, a president—without a party.

For all the noise and heat between Tyler and the Whigs on the topic of centralization versus states' rights, there were many more meaningful events of Tyler's presidency. The issue of Texas annexation moved closer to resolution as President Tyler took a firm stance that the United States had every right to annex that territory, and in fact, needed to for national security reasons. Tyler feared that if the United States did not move to annex Texas, the British would become more and more involved with it, to the eventual economic detriment of the United States. The British also angered Tyler, who after all, was a slaveholding Virginian, with their dedicated anti-slavery campaign carried out on the high seas by the British navy.

Having further potential to alienate Americans from the British was the continuing situation along the United States–Canadian border. The *Caroline* episode was still largely unresolved and hard feelings still predominated, especially between citizens of New York State and their neighbors to the north. Tyler handled all these issues with strength and skill, proving, to the surprise of many, to be an able and strong president. Nevertheless, he remained alienated from the parties and after the election of 1844, did not enter politics again until he was elected to the Confederate House of Representatives in 1861. He died, however, the next year, shortly before being sworn into office.

PRESIDENTIAL SUCCESSION

No one was quite sure how Vice President John Tyler should go about the duties of a president once Harrison died. Everyone knew that the office of vice president existed for a situation just such as this, but the transfer of power had never happened, and, as in many of its other provisions, the Constitution was a bit vague in explaining whether or not the vice president would actually assume all the powers of the presidency or would simply "hold" the office until the next election.

The first clue that John Tyler gave as to his views came when he insisted on giving his own inaugural address. He believed that he was assuming the presidency wholeheartedly, and would have every authority to take into his hands the reins of policy. He would not be the "acting" president; he was the president.

Those who opposed Tyler, either personally or his policies, were against such a course from the start. Many Whigs who had assented to his inclusion on the ticket felt strongly that Tyler ought to be bound to support the policies of the man who had been elected president, and that had been Harrison—not him. Opponents of Tyler as full president began referring to him as "His Accidency," particularly after it became clear that Tyler would neither adopt Harrison's policies as his own nor would he roll over and give in to anything Congress wanted to do. Others persisted in referring to his as the acting president or, more tellingly, still called him Vice President Tyler. Some demanded that he pledge not to run for reelection. He would have none of this. States' rights advocates, on the other hand, who had criticized Tyler first when he abandoned the Democrats and then more when he joined the Harrison ticket, were surprised and pleased at his forcefulness in office, but Whig criticism grew.

Tyler set an important precedent by assuming the full powers and titles of the presidency. He did not have to take the position he did, but in so doing, he took perhaps his most important and long-lasting action as president, setting the policy for every other vice president who found himself thrust up to the nation's highest office. The first excerpt here, from Tyler's inaugural address, makes it clear that Tyler is thinking of himself as nothing less than the actual president, imbued with all the powers of that office by virtue of the Constitution and his just being officially sworn in.

The contrary positions were usually very subtle, and are exemplified here by two passages from letters of Henry Clay. One was written the day of Tyler's inaugural, five days after the death of President Harrison. His repeated reference to "vice president" Tyler is too thoughtful to be the residue of mere habit, especially since he is talking about what Tyler will do in the future. The second letter is from over two years later, when Tyler's actions have angered Clay and other Whigs. Here the feeling toward his being president is even more clear.

FROM TYLER'S *INAUGURAL ADDRESS*, APRIL 9, 1841

Fellow Citizens: Before my arrival at the seat of Government the painful communication was made to you by officers presiding over the several Departments of the deeply regretted death of William Henry Harrison, late President of the United States. Upon him you had conferred your suffrages for the first office in your gift, and had selected his as your chosen instrument to correct and reform all such errors and abuses as had manifested themselves from time to time in the practical operation of the Government. While standing at the threshold of this great work he has by the dispensation of an all-wise Providence been removed from amongst us, and by the provisions of the Constitution the efforts to be directed to the accomplishing of this vitally important task have devolved upon myself. This same occurrence has subjected the wisdom and sufficiency of our institutions to a new test. For the first time in our history the person elected to the Vice-Presidency of the United States, by the happening of a contingency provided for in the Constitution, has had devolved upon him the Presidential office. The spirit of faction, which is directly opposed to the spirit of a lofty patriotism, may find in this occasion for assaults upon my Administration; and in succeeding, under circumstances so sudden and unexpected and to responsibilities so greatly augmented, to the administration of public affairs I shall place in the intelligence and patriotism of the people my only sure reliance. My earnest prayer shall be constantly addressed to the all-wise and all-powerful Being who made me, and by whose dispensation I am called to the high office of President of this Confederacy, understandingly to carry out the principles of that Constitution which I have sworn "to protect, preserve, and defend."

See *Messages and Papers of the Presidents* (New York: Bureau of National Literature, 1897), 4:1889–92.

Against Tyler's Formal Succession

HENRY CLAY TO JAMES F. CONOVER, APRIL 9, 1841

The distressing intelligence of the death of Genl. Harrison has reached me. It is greatly to be deplored, although it does not surprise me much, from what I observed of his habits and excitement.

. . . The best and most amicable relations exist between the Vice President and myself; but what his course will be I can only conjecture. . . . V.P. Tyler will, I presume, not confine the patronage of the Govt. exclusively to any particular class of the Whigs.

See Robert Seager II, ed., *The Papers of Henry Clay*, vol. 9, *The Whig Leader* (Lexington: University Press of Kentucky, 1984), 518.

HENRY CLAY TO JOHN M. BERRIEN, DECEMBER 9, 1843

. . . The truth is, that the public interest would not suffer, if the places which persons have recently been sent abroad to fill, were to remain unoccupied, during the residue of Mr Tyler's term. The acting President leaves vacant foreign appointments as in the instance of the French mission whenever he pleases.

See Robert Seager II, ed., *The Papers of Henry Clay*, vol. 9, *The Whig Leader* (Lexington: University Press of Kentucky, 1984), 900.

TARIFF POLICY

Regions of the country continued to be bitterly divided on the legitimacy of a tariff as the administration of William Henry Harrison, and then John Tyler, took office. Congressional delegations from agricultural states still tenaciously opposed them, while they remained absolutely necessary in the eyes of many northern states. The Whig Party (excluding most southern Whigs, who were really just Whigs in name only) believed tariffs were elemental in any sort of dynamic national economic policy that had as one of its major goals the building up of American industry. In the Whig interpretation of events, various manufactured goods from Europe, and from England especially, where the process of industrialization was much further along and more efficient, came into the United States at a cost far below what domestic manufacturers could charge. A tariff to make imports more expensive was the only way American factories felt they could compete, and in some instances, even survive.

But agricultural states with no factories saw only higher prices for manufactured goods they had to have. What was even more troublesome, when the United States put a tariff into effect, other countries often retaliated by putting a tariff on imports from America. The only material that the United States exported in any appreciable amount was the agricultural produce of these very same states—more often than not, cotton. So southern states, hurt in two directions by high tariff policies, determined to fight them. The more populous states of the North, however, could get such laws passed in the House of Representatives where they held an edge. Not only was sectional conflict over this issue inevitable; conflict between Tyler and Congress was as well.

The new administration had inherited a significant debt from President Van Buren, and Tyler was painfully aware that the treasury was nearly bare. Over the course of 1841, Tyler was forced to temporarily suspend payments to civil service workers and the military because of the crisis. He became aware of the need for a tariff for general revenue, but was increasingly troubled by Whig insistence that tariff policy be tied to a plan to sell off public lands and distribute the revenue to the states. Not only would this strengthen the Whig Party in the eyes of many; it would dangerously deplete what little resources the government had left. Tyler feared—and perhaps better, suspected—that such loss of assets would then legitimize Whig calls for even higher tariffs. Tyler therefore was determined that a bill creating a tariff for revenue would not pass his desk if it were tied to any other program.

For chronological reasons, and for reasons that will be obvious upon the reading of these two passages, the position against that ultimately assumed by the president is presented first, followed by that of Tyler.

Against Tyler's Tariff Position

In this excerpt from a letter to fellow Kentucky politician John Crittenden, Henry Clay lays out the problem created by too low a tariff or the lack of one. He explains the need for protection, as he calls it, in very concrete and practical terms that are often absent from more abstract political discussions of constitutionality and theory. Clearly, also, he is cognizant of what the opposition says about a tariff, as he is here voicing his certainty that it will indeed not make a final manufactured product more expensive for planters and thus limit its benefits to just one narrow slice of the society.

HENRY CLAY TO JOHN J. CRITTENDEN, JUNE 3, 1842

There is very great embarrassment and distress prevailing in K[entucky], much more than I imagined before I came home. . . . Most of our Hempen manufacturers are ruined, or menaced with ruin. Bagging and Rope were never known at any time heretofore to be so low as they are now. This is owing to the introduction of India and other foreign stuffs used as bagging. Our people say that they cannot do with less a protection than five Cents the square yard upon bagging. By the application of machinery to the spinning and weaving of the article, the cost of it is much reduced; and there is no danger of the planter being obliged to give a reasonable price for it. He is secure against that from the domestic competition. When the Tariff gets to the Senate (will it ever get there?) You and your colleague are expected to take care of this single Kentucky manufacture.

See Robert Seager II, ed., *The Papers of Henry Clay*, vol. 9, *The Whig Leader* (Lexington: University Press of Kentucky, 1984), 706.

TYLER'S VETO MESSAGE, JUNE 29, 1842

. . . [H]owever sensible I may be of the embarrassments to which the Executive, in the absence of all aid from the superior wisdom of the Legislature, will be liable in the enforcement of the existing laws, I have not, with the sincerest wish to acquiesce in the expressed will, been able to persuade myself that the exigency of the occasion is so great as to justify me in signing the bill in question with my present views of its character and effects. The existing laws, as I am advised, are sufficient to authorize and enable the collecting officers, under the directions of the Secretary of the Treasury, to levy the duties imposed by the act of 1833.

That act was passed under peculiar circumstances, to which it is not necessary that I should do more than barely allude. Whatever may be, in theory, its character, I have always regarded it as importing the highest moral obligation. It has now existed for nine years unchanged in any essential particular, with as general acquiescence, it is believed, of the whole country as that country has ever manifested for any of her wisely established institutions. It has insured to it the repose which always flows from truly wise and moderate counsels—a repose the more striking because of the long and angry agitations which preceded it. This salutary law proclaims in express terms the principle which, while it led to the abandonment of a scheme of indirect taxation founded on a false basis and pushed to dangerous excess, justifies any enlargement of duties that may be called for by the real exigencies of the public service.

. . . The bill assumes that a distribution of the proceeds of the public lands is, by existing laws, to be made on the 1st day of July, 1842, notwithstanding there has been an imposition of duties on imports exceeding 20 per cent up to that day, and directs it to be made on the 1st of August next. It seems to be very clear that this conclusion is equally erroneous and dangerous, as it would divert from the Treasury a fund sacredly pledged for the general purposes of the Government is the event of a rate of duty above 20 per cent being found necessary for an economical administration of the Government.

The bill under consideration is designed only as a temporary measure; and thus a temporary measure, passed merely for the convenience of Congress, is made to affect the vital principle of an important act. . . . I see enough in it to justify me in adhering to the law as it stands in preference to subjecting a condition so vitally affecting the peace of the country, and so solemnly enacted at a momentous crisis, and so steadfastly adhered to ever since, and so replete, if adhered to, with good to every interest of the country, to doubtful or captious interpretation.

See *Messages and Papers of the Presidents* (New York: Bureau of National Literature, 1897), 5:2033–36.

THE BANK

Like Democrats everywhere, John Tyler opposed a national bank and he made his opinions well known throughout his career. Once he became president, Tyler had to face a determined Henry Clay, who intended to push through legislation recreating the Bank of the United States, believing that the new president would not veto it.

The arguments in large part remained the same as they had been in the day of Andrew Jackson. For Tyler, it was a question of legitimate powers of the government being augmented by illegitimate ones. Congress had no power to create a bank, therefore doing so was a dangerous and troublesome precedent, especially in the understanding of a states' rights man like himself. That other presidents had believed it possible and constitutional had no bearing on what he saw himself as called to do.

In particular, Tyler was troubled by the provisions in the bill that required a state to go along with the national government—and the Bank— whenever the Bank wanted to open a branch office in that state. The right of a state to regulate its own affairs, therefore, was abrogated. A state's dissent meant nothing. The president could not endorse such an increase in the national government's power with the necessary corresponding decrease in that of the states'.

Henry Clay, as one would expect by this point, defends the legislation. The national government has to be able to require a state to fall in line in terms of bank branches. Not to have the power to do so in such an important element of the national monetary policy was to subordinate the good of the entire nation to the whims or prejudices of one particular state. In Clay's estimation, what would result in such an arrangement would not, in fact, be a nation. The national government could not be dependent on any subset of the nation for its action.

TYLER'S BANK VETO MESSAGE, AUGUST 16, 1841

. . . The power of Congress to create a national bank to operate per se over the Union has been a question of dispute from the origin of the Government. Men most justly and deservedly esteemed for their high intellectual endowments, their virtue, and their patriotism have in regard to it entertained different and conflicting opinions; Congresses have differed; the approval of one President has been followed by the disapproval of another; the people at different times have acquiesced in decisions both for and against. The country has been and still is deeply agitated by this unsettled question. It will suffice for me to say that my own opinion has been uniformly proclaimed to be against the exercise of any such power by this Government.

. . . Without going further into the argument, I will say that in looking to the powers of this Government to collect, safely keep, and disburse the public revenue, and incidentally to regulate the commerce and exchanges, I have not been able to satisfy myself that the establishment by this Government of a bank of discount in the ordinary acceptation of that term was a necessary means or one demanded by propriety to execute those powers.

. . . On general principles the right in Congress to prescribe terms to any State implies a superiority of power and control, deprives the transaction of all pretense to compact between them, and terminates, as we have seen, in the total abrogation of freedom of action on the part of the States. But, further, the State may express, after the most solemn form of legislation, its dissent, which may from time to time thereafter be repeated in full view of its own interest, which can never be separated from the wise and beneficent operation of this Government, and yet Congress may by virtue of the last proviso overrule its law, and upon grounds which to such State will appear to rest on a constructive necessity and propriety and nothing more. I regard the bill as asserting for Congress the right to incorporate a United States bank with power and right to establish offices of discount and deposit in the several States of this Union with or without their consent—a principle to which I have always heretofore been opposed and which can never obtain my sanction; and waiving all other considerations growing out of its other provisions, I return it to the House in which it originated with these my objections to its approval.

See *Messages and Papers of the Presidents* (New York: Bureau of National Literature, 1897), 4:1916–21.

Against Tyler's Position

HENRY CLAY, SPEECH IN SENATE, JUNE 1841

A derivation of power to the General Government from the consent of particular States would be unsound in principle, and the committee apprehend dangerous in practice. Admit such consent to be a legitimate source of power, the Government would not operate equally in all the States, and the Constitution, losing its uniform character, would exhibit an irregular and incongruous action. Entertaining these deliberate views, the committee are decidedly of opinion that no bill for the establishment of a Bank in the District of Columbia will be effectual which does not contain a clear recognition of the constitutional power of Congress to establish branches wherever, in the United States, the public wants, in its judgment, require them. They cannot consent that a Bank, emanating from the will of the nation, and imperatively demanded by the necessities of the Government and of the nation, shall be wholly dependent for its useful operation upon the will of each and every State, distinctly expressed.

. . . If it be true that money is power, its concentration under the direction of one will, sole or collective, must augment the power. A nation, without such a concentration of power, maintaining extensive commercial intercourse with another nation possessing it, must conduct that intercourse on a condition of inequality and disadvantage. National Banks, in other countries, beget the necessity, therefore, of a National Bank in this country, in like manner as National Governments in foreign nations must be met by a National Government in ours.

See Robert Seager II, ed., *The Papers of Henry Clay*, vol. 9, *The Whig Leader* (Lexington: University Press of Kentucky, 1984), 549–50.

THE SLAVE TRADE

As far as slavery was concerned, the primary goal of politicians who were not abolitionists was to keep the topic out of public discourse. A gag rule to that effect had even been passed in the House of Representatives, to the disgust and dismay of many northerners.

The onset of the British campaign to wipe out the slave trade, however, presented a fresh challenge to the practice of keeping quiet any talk of the government's position on slavery. The Constitution had made it possible for Congress to outlaw the importation of slavers after a certain year, and once it could, it had immediately done so. The British, however, after having outlawed slavery in all their colonies in 1833, were taking things a step further with their active suppression by means of their navy, of the slave trade carried on by anyone, anywhere on the high seas. Abolitionists in the United States hailed the effort, but slaveholders and likeminded politicians gave little more than faint praise to the cause.

As president, Tyler had to defend the sanctity of American shipping against what seemed to many to be utter capriciousness on the part of the British navy in repeated instances in which British ships stopped and searched American ones. Tyler had enough rhetorical freedom to condemn the slave trade in general terms as an affront to humanity, but he essentially put American maritime rights over the morality that underlay the British effort.

Frederick Douglass, on the other hand, praised the British for their work in ending slavery, and completely endorsed any and all efforts to stamp out the institution wherever it existed. The cause of freedom was too important (yet slavery was too ingrained in the American fabric) to rely on any one nation to take up the crusade by itself and hope for success. He also believed that a nation like the United States would have trouble exorcising slavery from within itself without help from the outside. He calls upon the British to exert ever more pressure on the United States to put an end to slavery once and for all.

FROM TYLER'S *FIRST ANNUAL MESSAGE TO CONGRESS*, DECEMBER 7, 1841

. . . Our commercial interests in that region [off the coast of Africa] have experienced considerable increase and have become an object of much importance, and it is the duty of this Government to protect them against all improper and vexatious interruption. However desirous the United States may be for the suppression of the slave trade, they can not consent to interpolations into the maritime code at the mere will and pleasure of other governments. We deny the right of any such interpolation to any one or all the nations of the earth without our consent. We claim to have a voice in all amendments or alterations of that code, and when we are given to understand, as in this instance, by a foreign government that its treaties with other nations can not be executed without the establishment and enforcement of new principles of maritime police, to be applied without our consent, we must employ a language neither of equivocal import or susceptible of misconstruction. American citizens prosecuting a lawful commerce in the African seas under the flag of their country are not responsible for the abuse or unlawful use of that flag by others; nor can they rightfully on account of any such alleged abuses be interrupted, molested, or detained while on the ocean, and if thus molested and detained while pursuing honest voyages in the usual way and violating no law themselves they are unquestionably entitled to indemnity. This Government has manifested its repugnance to the slave trade in a manner which can not be misunderstood. . . . Whether this Government should now enter into treaties containing mutual stipulations upon this subject is a question for its mature deliberation. Certain it is that if the right to detain American ships on the high seas can be justified on the plea of a necessity for such detention arising out of the existence of treaties between other nations, the same plea may be extended and enlarged by the new stipulations of new treaties to which the United States may not be a party. This Government will not cease to urge upon that of Great Britain full and ample remuneration for all losses, whether arising from detention or otherwise, to which American citizens have heretofore been or may hereafter be subjected by the exercise of rights which this Government can not recognize as legitimate and proper. Nor will I indulge a doubt but that the sense of justice of Great Britain will constrain her to make retribution for a wrong or loss which any American citizen engaged in the prosecution of lawful commerce may have experienced at the hands of her cruisers or other public authorities. This Government, at the same time, will relax no effort to prevent its citizens, if there be any so disposed, from prosecuting a traffic so revolting to the feelings of humanity. It seeks to do no more than to protect the fair and honest trader from molestation and injury; but while the enterprising mariner engaged in the pursuit of an honorable trade is entitled to its protection, it will visit with condign punishment others of an opposite character.

See *Messages and Papers of the Presidents* (New York: Bureau of National Literature, 1897), 4:1927–42.

Against Tyler's Position

FREDERICK DOUGLASS, SPEECH AT MOORFIELDS, ENGLAND, MAY 12, 1846

I feel exceedingly glad of the opportunity now afforded me of presenting the claims of my brethren in bonds in the United States, to so many in London and from various parts of Britain, who have assembled here on the present occasion. . . . I will take it for granted that you know something about the degrading influences of slavery, and that you will not expect great things from me this evening, but simply such facts as I may be able to advance immediately in connection with my own experience of slavery.

. . . I may be asked, why I am so anxious to bring this subject before the British public—why I do not confine my efforts to the United States? My answer is, first, that slavery is the common enemy of mankind, and all mankind should be made acquainted with its abominable character. My next answer is, that the slave is a man, and, as such, is entitled to your sympathy as a brother. All the feelings, all the susceptibilities, all the capacities, which you have, he has. He is a part of the human family. . . . I have another reason for bringing this matter before the British public, and it is this: slavery is a system of wrong, so blinding to all around, so hardening to the heart, so corrupting to the morals, so deleterious to religion, so sapping to all the principles of justice in its immediate vicinity, that the community surrounding it lack the moral stamina necessary to its removal. It is a system of such gigantic evil, so strong, so overwhelming in its power, that no one nation is equal to its removal. It requires the humanity of christianity, the morality of the world to remove it. Hence, I call upon the people of Britain to look at this matter, and to exert the influence I am about to show they possess, for the removal of slavery from America. I can appeal to them, as strongly by their regard for the slaveholder as for the slave, to labor in this cause. I am here, because you have an influence on America that no other nation can have. . . . There is nothing said here against slavery that will not be recorded in the United States. I am here, also, because the slaveholders do not want me to be here; they would rather that I were not here.

. . . To tear off the mask from this abominable system, to expose it to the light of heaven, aye, to the heat of the sun, that it may burn and wither it out of existence, is my object in coming to this country. I want the slaveholder surrounded, as by a wall of anti-slavery fire, so that he may see the condemnation of himself and his system glaring down in letters of light. I want him to feel that he has no sympathy in England, Scotland, or Ireland; that he has none in Canada, none in Mexico, none among the poor wild Indians; that the voice of the civilized, aye, and savage world is against him. I would have condemnation blaze down upon him in every direction, till, stunned and overwhelmed with shame and confusion, he is compelled to let go the grasp he holds upon the persons of his victims, and restore them to their long-lost rights.

See http://www.yale.edu/glc/archive/1077.htm.

THE *CAROLINE* AFFAIR

What had become known in the United States, Canada, and Great Britain during Martin Van Buren's administration as the *Caroline* Affair remained unresolved well into the 1840s. Repeated diplomatic efforts to keep the peace between the United States and British Canada had kept the governments from breaking relations and going to war, but tensions between Washington and London still ran high, due to the unsettled nature of the border troubles. Few Americans felt sympathy for the British in their struggle to keep hold of Canada, while many felt a natural brotherhood with those in Canada wanting independence.

In President Tyler's First Annual Address to Congress, he lamented that the United States still had not received the kind of consideration his administration demanded from London. There had been no reparations for the property damaged during the raid that sent the blazing ship *Caroline* over Niagara Falls, and no formal apology. Such willful disregard of the proper conduct between independent nations, Tyler believed, reflected poorly on the British government and even more poorly on the American government's ability to demand respect and equal treatment from other nations. He could not allow a violation of sovereign territory, such as had occurred when the *Caroline* was attacked, to go unchecked and unchallenged, for diplomatic ruin was surely the consequence of such a course.

In a letter to Secretary of State Daniel Webster, British foreign secretary Lord Ashburton explained why the British government felt it had to take the action it did. While not surrendering his government's authority to chase down and punish such terrorists as had been staging raids from American soil into Canada, he hopes that the United States and Britain can somehow keep on good terms.

FROM TYLER'S *FIRST ANNUAL MESSAGE TO CONGRESS*, DECEMBER 7, 1841

. . . I regret that it is not in my power to make known to you [a] . . . satisfactory conclusion in the case of the *Caroline* steamer, with the circumstances connected with the destruction of which, in December, 1837, by an armed force fitted out in the Province of Upper Canada, you are already made acquainted. No such atonement as was due for the public wrong done to the United States by this invasion of her territory, so wholly irreconcilable with her rights as an independent power, has yet been made. In the view taken by this Government the inquiry whether the vessel was in the employment of those who were prosecuting an unauthorized war against that Province or was engaged by the owner in the business of transporting passengers to and from Navy Island in hopes of private gain, which was most probably the case, in no degree alters the real question at issue between the two Governments. This government can never concede to any foreign government the power, except in a case of the most urgent and extreme necessity, of invading its territory, either to arrest the persons or destroy the property of those who may have violated the municipal laws of such foreign government or have disregarded their obligations arising under the law of nations. The territory of the United States must be regarded as sacredly secure against all such invasions until they shall voluntarily acknowledge their inability to acquit themselves of their duties to others. . . . To recognize it as an admissible practice that each Government in its turn, upon any sudden and unauthorized outbreak which, on a frontier the extent of which renders it impossible for either to have an efficient force on every mile of it, and which outbreak, therefore, neither may be able to suppress in a day, may take vengeance into its own hands, and without even a remonstrance, and in the absence of any pressing or overruling necessity may invade the territory of the other, would inevitably lead to results equally to be deplored by both. When border collisions come to receive the sanction or to be made or the authority of either Government general war must be the inevitable result. While it is the ardent desire of the United States to cultivate the relations of peace with all nations and to fulfill all the duties of good neighborhood toward those who possess territories adjoining their own, that very desire would lead them to deny the right of any foreign power to invade their boundary with an armed force.

See *Messages and Papers of the Presidents* (New York: Bureau of National Literature, 1897), 4:1927–42.

The English Position

LORD ASHBURTON TO SECRETARY OF STATE DANIEL WEBSTER, JULY 28, 1842

. . . Every consideration . . . leads us to set as highly as your Government can possibly do this paramount obligation of reciprocal respect for the independent territory of each. But however strong this duty may be it is admitted by all writers, by all Jurists, by the occasional practice of all nations, not excepting your own, that a strong overpowering necessity may arise, when this great principle may and must be suspended. It must be so for the shortest possible period, during the continuance of an admitted overruling necessity, and strictly confined within the narrowest limits imposed by that necessity. Self defence is the first law of our nature and it must be recognized by every code which professes to regulate the condition and relations of man.

... But the case we are considering is of a wholly different description, and may be best determined by answering the following question. Supposing a man standing on ground where you have no legal right to follow him has a weapon long enough to reach you, and is striking you down and endangering your life, How long are you bound to wait for the assistance of the authority having the legal power to relieve your or, to bring the facts more immediately home to the ease, if cannon are moving and setting up in a battery which can reach you and are actually destroying life and property by their fire, If you have remonstrated for some time without effect and see no prospect of relief, when begins your right to defend yourself, should you have no other means of doing so, than by seizing your assailant on the verge of a neutral territory?

... Remonstrances, wholly ineffectual were made; so ineffectual indeed that a Militia regiment, stationed on the neighbouring American island, looked on without any attempt at interference, while shots were fired from the American island itself. ... This force, formed of all the reckless and mischievous people of the border, formidable from their numbers and from their armament, had in their pay and as part of their establishment this steamboat *Caroline*, the important means and instrument by which numbers and arms were hourly increasing. I might safely put it to any candid man acquainted with the existing state of things, to say whether the military commander in Canada had the remotest reason on the 29th of December to expect to be relieved from this state of suffering by the protective intervention of any American authority. How long could a Government, having the paramount duty of protecting its own people be reasonably expected to wait for what they had then no reason to expect?

... I have only further to notice the highly coloured picture drawn in your note of the facts attending the execution of this service. Some importance is attached to the attack having been made in the night and the vessel having been set on fire and floated down the falls of the river, and it is insinuated rather than asserted that there was carelessness as to the lives of the persons on board. The account given by the distinguished officer who commanded the expedition distinctly refutes or satisfactorily explains these assertions. The time of night was purposely selected as most likely to ensure the execution with the least loss of life, and it is expressly stated that, the strength of the current not permitting the vessel to be carried off, and it being necessary to destroy her by fire, she was drawn into the stream for the express purpose of preventing injury to persons or property of the inhabitants at Schlosser.

... Although it is believed that a candid and impartial consideration of the whole history of this unfortunate event will lead to the conclusion that there were grounds of justification as strong as were ever presented in such cases, and above all that no slight of the authority of the United States was ever intended, yet it must be admitted that there was in the hurried execution of this necessary service a violation of territory, and I am instructed to assure you that Her Majesty's Government consider this as a most serious fact, that far from thinking that an event of this kind should be lightly risked, they would unfeignedly deprecate its recurrence.

This message, along with many other documents on the *Caroline* Affair and the Tyler administration's actions regarding it, can be found at http://www.yale.edu/lawweb/avalon/diplomacy/britian/br-1842d.htm.

THE ANNEXATION OF TEXAS

The question of whether the United States should or should not annex the Republic of Texas had gone on almost since the end of the Texas Revolution in 1836. Many politicians, especially from the South, had repeatedly all but demanded annexation, but the presidents had stepped clear of the issue, knowing full well how controversial it was in relation to slavery and the expansion of the slaveholding South. The Tyler administration took a slightly different tack. Tyler thought that the United States should annex Texas, and once he had definitively broken ranks with the Whig Party over the Bank issue, he began moving openly in a pro-annexation direction. In doing so, he reflected what seemed to be a growing interest in Texas in the country at large. The lure of expansion and Manifest Destiny was taking hold of Americans' imagination, and it looked all but inevitable that Texas would someday join the union on its irresistible march westward. "Texas Fever," it was called.

It was not until the eleventh hour of Tyler's administration that Congress finally took action. Eschewing the more formal legislative route, the Senate and House of Representatives took the easier way by simply passing a Joint Resolution announcing that Texas was now part of the union. President Tyler, however, had endorsed the cause almost a year earlier in his message to Congress in April 1844.

FROM TYLER'S *MESSAGE TO THE SENATE OF THE UNITED STATES*, APRIL 22, 1844

I transmit herewith, for your approval and ratification, a treaty which I have caused to be negotiated between the United States and Texas, whereby the latter, on the conditions therein set forth, has transferred and conveyed all its right of separate and independent sovereignty and jurisdiction to the United States. In taking so important a step I have been influenced by what appeared to me to be the most controlling considerations of public policy and the general good, and in having accomplished it, should it meet with your approval, the Government will have succeeded in reclaiming a territory which formerly constituted a portion, as it is confidently believed, of its domain under the treaty of cession of 1803 by France to the United States.

The country thus proposed to be annexed has been settled principally by persons from the United States, who emigrated on the invitation of both Spain and Mexico, and who carried with them into the wilderness which they have partially reclaimed the laws, customs, and political and domestic institutions of their native land. They are deeply indoctrinated in all the principles of civil liberty, and will bring along with them in the act of reassociation devotion to our Union and a firm and inflexible resolution to assist in maintaining the public liberty unimpaired—a consideration which, as it appears to me, is to be regarded as of no small moment. The country itself thus obtained is of incalculable value in an agricultural and commercial point of view. To a soil of inexhaustible fertility it unites a genial and healthy climate, and is destined at a day not distant to make large contributions to the commerce of the world.

. . . Texas voluntarily steps forth, upon terms of perfect honor and good faith to all nations, to ask to be annexed to the Union. As an independent sovereignty her right to do this is unquestionable. In doing so she gives no cause of umbrage to any other power; her people desire it, and there is no slavish transfer of her sovereignty and independence. She has for eight years maintained her independence against all efforts to subdue her. She has been recognized as independent by many of the most prominent of the family of nations, and that recognition, so far as they are concerned, places her in a position, without giving any just cause of umbrage to them, to surrender her sovereignty at her own will and pleasure. . . . Our right to receive the rich grant tendered by Texas is perfect, and this Government should not, having due respect either to its own honor or its own interests, permit its course of policy to be interrupted by the interference of other powers, even if such interference were threatened.

. . . There is no desire on the part of the Executive to wound [the government of Mexico's] pride or affect injuriously her interest, but at the same time it can not compromit by any delay in its action the essential interests of the United States. Mexico has no right to ask or expect this of us; we deal rightfully with Texas as an independent power. The war which has been waged for eight years has resulted only in the conviction with all others than herself that Texas can not be reconquered. . . . I repeat, the Executive saw Texas in a state of almost hopeless exhaustion, and the question was narrowed down to the simple proposition whether the United States should accept the boon of annexation upon fair and even liberal terms, or, by refusing to do so, force Texas to seek refuge in the arms of some other power, either through a treaty of alliance, offensive and defensive, or the adoption of some other expedient which might virtually make her tributary to such power and dependent upon it for all future time. The Executive has full reason to believe that such would have been the result without its interposition, and that such will be the result in the event either of unnecessary delay in the ratification or of the rejection of the proposed treaty.

See *Messages and Papers of the Presidents* (New York: Bureau of National Literature, 1897), 5:2160–66.

Against Tyler's Position on Texas

AN APPEAL TO THE PEOPLE OF MASSACHUSETTS ON THE TEXAS QUESTION

The course pursued by the Administration in reference to the annexation of Texas renders a crisis inevitable. . . . It is now clear that the only design of the measure—the *avowed* design, too—is, to fortify, extend, and perpetuate the slave-holding power; to insure the Slave-holding States the control of the General Government for all domestic purposes; and to make the General Government, in their hands, instrumental in effecting a foreign policy which shall place this country in immediate and constant hostility to England upon the great question of universal emancipation, and in reference to all measures and interests connected therewith.

Now, that this is a project as dangerous as it is wicked, and as alarming as it is bold, will be seen—and it may be presumed that it is already *seen* and *felt*—by the great mass of people in the Free States. The Message and its accompanying documents have scarcely yet reached the extremities of the Free States; but such was the prevailing anxiety in advance of their reception, that it cannot be doubted they will be universally and eagerly read at the earliest possible moment,—and that, as soon as they are read, there will be but one feeling in regard to what is about to be attempted by the Administration, and in respect to the duty, to the extent of what is practicable, of defeating such an attempt.

. . . With so many discouragements all around, and so many obstacles before us, let us still venture to ask and to answer the question,—WHAT IS OUR DUTY? Is it to cease from effort, because there is such necessity and so much scope for exertion? Is it to postpone any attempt which can only become the more hopeless the longer it is delayed? Is it to shut our eyes to the true state of the case, lest . . . a full view of our danger should make us feel that there is no alternative but a death-struggle? Is it to wait for others when we are ready to act? . . . No! No! Massachusetts must be Massachusetts still. Founded on the Rock of Plymouth, the strength of her character is moral and religious principle. Baptized in the fire and blood of the Revolution, her patriotism will abide every test, and prove itself ready for any crisis.

Broadside published in Boston by Charles C. Little and James Brown, 1844. Texas Collection, Baylor University, Waco, Texas.

LETTER FROM HENRY CLAY TO THE WASHINGTON *NATIONAL INTELLIGENCER*, APRIL 17, 1844

. . . I do not think that Texas ought to be received into the Union, as an integral part of it, in decided opposition to the wishes of a considerable and respectable portion of the confederacy. I think it far more wise and important to compose and harmonize the present confederacy, as it now exists, than to introduce a new element of discord and distraction into it.

It is useless to disguise that there are those who espouse and those who oppose the annexation of Texas upon the ground of the influence which it would exert, in the balance of political power, between two great sections of the Union. I conceive that no motive for the acquisition of foreign territory would be more unfortunate, or pregnant with more fatal consequences, than that of obtaining it for the purpose of strengthening one part against another part of the common confederacy. Such a principle, put into practical operation, would menace the existence, if it did not certainly sow the seeds of a dissolution of the Union. . . . For if today Texas be acquired to strengthen one part of the confederacy, to-morrow Canada may be required to add strength to the other.

. . . In conclusion, they may be stated in a few words to be, that I consider the annexation of Texas, at this time, without the assent of Mexico, as a measure compromising the national character, involving us certainly in war with Mexico, probably with other foreign powers, dangerous to the integrity of the Union, inexpedient in the present financial condition of the country, and not called for by any general expression of public opinion.

See Arthur M. Schlesinger Jr. et al., *History of American Presidential Elections, 1789–1968* (New York: Chelsea House, 1971), 2:816–17.

RECOMMENDED READINGS

Monroe, Dan. *The Republican Vision of John Tyler*. College Station: Texas A&M University Press, 2003.
Peterson, Merrill D. *The Great Triumvirate: Webster, Clay, and Calhoun*. New York: Oxford University Press, 1987.
Peterson, Norma Lois. *The Presidencies of William Henry Harrison and John Tyler*. Lawrence: University Press of Kansas, 1989.
Seager, Robert, II. *And Tyler, Too*. New York: McGraw-Hill, 1963.
Sellers, Charles. *The Market Revolution: Jacksonian America, 1815–1846*. New York: Oxford University Press, 1991.

5

JAMES K. POLK

(1845–1849)

"Who is James K. Polk?" asked the Whig Party derisively throughout the presidential campaign of 1844. Polk, the Democrat candidate for president, was a virtual unknown outside the party, and when the Democrats gathered in convention to choose their candidate, no one would have suspected that James Polk of Tennessee would emerge as their man. He had been in politics for quite a while, serving primarily in the House of Representatives, and was a loyal and ardent Jacksonian, but in terms of national reputation he could not hope to stand up against the venerable Henry Clay, whom the Whigs nominated for president. In truth, Polk had been a compromise candidate, chosen at the convention when the Democrats could not seem to agree on anyone else. He would emerge, however, as the most powerful and influential president between Jackson and Abraham Lincoln.

James Knox Polk was born in North Carolina in 1795 and moved with his family to Tennessee when he was about ten years old. After going back to his home state for college at the University of North Carolina, he returned to Tennessee and embarked on a career as a lawyer, at which he enjoyed marked success, success which encouraged him to enter politics. He won a seat in the Tennessee state legislature where he emerged as a dedicated and loyal follower of Andrew Jackson and his policies. Shortly thereafter, he won election to the U.S. Congress where he eventually served fourteen years, rising to the rank of Speaker of the House during the last years of Jackson's and the first years of Van Buren's administrations. In 1839 he returned to Tennessee to become governor. After two years in office, he failed to win reelection, and most people thought his political career was probably over.

But over the course of his years in politics, James K. Polk had made his reputation as a bold and partisan Democrat, made squarely in the mold of Jackson. So much in fact did Polk pattern his style and views on his mentor, he garnered the nickname "Young Hickory" or sometimes "Little Hickory," which alone made him memorable. As Democrats gathered for their presidential convention in 1844, many believed that Polk would make an ideal vice presidential candidate behind either former president Martin Van Buren or Senator Lewis Cass of Michigan. As events played out, however, supporters of Van Buren and supporters of Cass were deadlocked. Southerners would not support Van Buren because he had come out against the annexation of Texas, but likewise Cass could not gather enough support to make him the nominee. Ballot after ballot returned deadlocked results. Finally, Polk's name came forward as one who was an unapologetic proponent of expansion. The elderly Jackson, still revered as the architect of the party, encouraged Polk's candidacy, endorsed his views on national expansion, and the convention finally nominated "Young Hickory" for president.

Polk's campaign platform was rather simple: unabashed national territorial expansion behind which Democrats from both South and North could be expected to rally. He brought in northern proponents of expansion by promising to add the Oregon territory to the union, a skillful tactic to offset the distinctively southern appeal that his pledge to "re-annex" Texas had. "Re-annex," moreover, implied that for the United States to have Texas in the union would be less a brand new course of action than simply taking back what had been given away in the past. Although it was not a widely stated goal of any presumptive Polk administration, Polk personally wanted very much to add the Mexican territory of California to the union as well. Early on he was interested in purchasing California from the Mexican government, and was apparently willing to spend what it would take. When the Mexican government rebuffed these overtures, however, Polk's determination did not wane. He would simply have to find another means of adding that coastline to the union.

Extending American jurisdiction across the continent was becoming a popular fascination, and this reinforced Polk's own plans. The nation was in the emotional grip of "Manifest Destiny" as the election of 1844 approached. A term coined by a newspaperman, Manifest Destiny held that it was the God-given destiny, and therefore the right, of the United States to spread from the Atlantic Ocean to the Pacific. As Polk's Whig opponent Henry Clay, who was feeling the emotional pull of this idea on the American people, began to shift his position on the Texas question, doing so only turned abolitionists and those who categorically opposed expansion away from him and toward the new Liberty Party, which expressly promised to fight slavery. Polk narrowly won the election, and became the eleventh president.

Polk became president with many challenges looming before him, some of which were caused by the passionate rhetoric of Manifest Destiny. The future of the Oregon country, which for years had been jointly occupied by both the United States and Great Britain, was one such challenge. By the time of the election of 1844, the idea of Manifest Destiny had created a "whole of Oregon" movement that believed the United States should demand Britain abandon all of its claims to the region. The northern boundary of Oregon, which was also the southern boundary of Russian Alaska, was latitude 54° 40', which led to the memorable slogan "54° 40' or Fight!" emerging shortly after Polk took office. It implied that the United States should unilaterally take all of the Oregon territory and be willing to fight Great Britain for it. Polk did nothing to squelch such rhetoric, and while as a candidate he had doubted the wisdom of the "whole of Oregon" movement, whether he would be willing to go to war with Great Britain over the entirety of the Oregon territory remained to be seen.

Just before Polk took office, Congress passed a joint resolution annexing Texas, giving to the incoming Polk administration the distinct possibility of war with Mexico, which since Texas independence in 1836 had repeatedly invaded what it still apparently considered a renegade province. By no means was Polk going to shrink away from a challenge from the Mexican government, and its threats of war would not dissuade him from using all his power as president to protect what was now a part of the United States. As far as California was concerned, Polk began approaching Mexico shortly after his inauguration with offers to purchase the territory.

As far as other domestic issues were concerned, issues that had nothing to do with expansion, Polk reflected the typical positions of other Democrats. He was for a lower tariff, and he was determined to keep slavery out of public discourse—and in terms of formal policy, do nothing to touch it where it existed. He was also for the independent treasury, over which politicians had been fighting since the demise of the Second Bank of the United States under Andrew Jackson, and which had been cancelled by the Whigs in 1841 after only a few months in existence. Finally, as had his mentor Jackson, Polk was not reluctant to use the power of the veto to prevent spending on internal improvements. Time and time again when such bills came to his desk, they found his veto pen waiting.

The determination with which Polk faced his domestic agenda was bolstered by other issues that were beginning to force relatively bland topics like the tariff and the independent treasury plan to the sidelines. As more heated questions fired newly passionate debates, Congress and, more particularly, the public were not able to marshal as much energy to debate tariffs, for instance. Slavery and territorial expansion were the two main reasons of this gradual redirection of public debate. And ironically, due to Polk's success in the latter, the two issues unexpectedly became intertwined and therefore wielded a stronger grip on the public imagination.

The abolitionist movement continued to grow in the 1840s and linked itself to the question of national expansion over the annexation of Texas. Just a year after annexation, in 1846, Pennsylvania congressman David Wilmot introduced a resolution that came to be called the Wilmot Proviso, stipulating that slavery would not be allowed in any of the territories that the United States may acquire as a result of the Mexican War. Even though it was voted down, the Wilmot Proviso brought to a sudden end the attempt to keep slavery out of public discourse by focusing on Manifest Destiny instead.

When James K. Polk left office four years after his inaugural, he left a very different United States with a very different map. Polk's determination to have Oregon, California, and Texas resulted in a nation that now stretched from the Atlantic to the Pacific, and encompassed the forests of the Pacific Northwest and the deserts of the Southwest. Puget Sound in Oregon and San Francisco Bay in California gave the country the two best harbors on the west coast of North America from which to extend the American presence into the Pacific and send the country's merchant ships to tap the economic potential of the China market.

On the domestic front, no longer were economic issues like tariffs and banks at the core of presidential campaigns. Now it was slavery: its expansion in particular. This would remain front and center in the national debate, requiring one last compromise to be put together by the indefatigable Henry Clay in 1850. It would not last long, though. By the time Polk left office, a perceptible slide had begun that would carry the nation irresistibly toward a war to settle the question of slavery and of states' rights once and for all.

Two questions that had dominated the attention of the second generation of American politicians would soon be put to rest. Polk, however, would not live to see it. He died in June 1849, just a few months after leaving office.

CALIFORNIA

President Polk's desire for the United States to have a presence on the West Coast was nothing new. Thomas Jefferson, for instance, had sent Lewis and Clark across the continent not just for exploration, but to find a passage to the Pacific so that the trade of China might be made to flow across the North American continent. One of the first tasks that expedition set about to do when reaching the ocean was to build a fort. An awareness of the benefits of having a Pacific presence had been a clear idea for a long time. The administration of James K. Polk, however, marked a turning point. Polk's determination to take action is what set him apart from his predecessors.

The level of control that the Mexican government exerted over California—or Upper California, as it was known to Mexico—was a question of some debate. What was not debated was that every year there were more American citizens moving westward to California. Many of these first arrived on the West Coast on merchant ships from New York or Boston that regularly traded hides and tallow with the enormous ranches that dotted the coastline from San Diego to San Francisco. Others crossed over to California via wagon trains on the California Trail. By 1843, a settlement at the confluence of the American River and the Sacramento River called Sutter's Fort was attracting numerous settlers from the United States. By the middle of the decade there were hundreds of Americans in California.

In the wake of the Texas Revolution, many in the United States assumed that such would be the inevitable course followed by California: An influx of settlers from the United States, a sudden revolution, and then independence. The technical question would then be the same as that in the Texas case: Does the Constitution provide for the annexing of an independent state? To be sure, given California's economy and social structure, slavery would not figure into the equation in the same way as in Texas, so perhaps there would not be as much indecision. But on the other hand, a revolution in California might be a long time in coming, and perhaps it might not come at all.

Whatever the future held, by the early 1840s it seemed as though something was bound to happen soon. There was much talk in Congress about British and French interest in California, and worry over American involvement lagging behind that of these two commercial competitors. There was the nagging question of just what action the British or French would take if a revolution did break out. In October 1845, President Polk instructed Thomas Larkin, the consul in Monterey, the capital of California, to talk up the close ties that could and should exist between the region and the United States, while the next month, Polk put yet another piece of his plan into motion.

Another option for the president, if he really wanted California, was to attempt an outright purchase of the territory. To this end, Polk dispatched a special minister to Mexico, John Slidell, who was authorized to offer that government up to $20 million if it would sell California to the United States. Slidell could also offer to settle any and all damage claims that Mexico had against the United States. It turned him down cold. Shortly after receiving news of this, Polk ordered General Zachary Taylor's army, stationed along the coast of Texas in Corpus Christi, to move southward toward the Rio Grande, the river that the Americans and Texans held as the boundary of the United States and Mexico.

FROM POLK'S *THIRD ANNUAL MESSAGE TO CONGRESS*, DECEMBER 7, 1847

... The cession to the United States by Mexico of the Provinces of New Mexico and the Californias, as proposed by the commissioner of the United States, it was believed would be more in accordance with the convenience and interests of both nations than any other cession of territory which it was probable Mexico could be induced to make.

It is manifest to all who have observed the actual condition of the Mexican Government for some years past and at present that if these Provinces should be retained by her she could not long continue to hold and govern them. Mexico is too feeble a power to govern these Provinces, lying as they do at a distance of more than 1,000 miles from her capital, and if attempted to be retained by her they would constitute but for a short time even nominally a part of her dominions. This would be especially the case with Upper California.

The sagacity of powerful European nations has long since directed their attention to the commercial importance of that Province, and there can be little doubt that the moment the United States shall relinquish their present occupation of it and their claim to it as indemnity an effort would be made by some foreign power to possess it, either by conquest or by purchase. If no foreign government should acquire it in either of these modes, an independent revolutionary government would probably be established by the inhabitants and such foreigners as may remain in or remove to the country as soon as it shall be known that the United States have abandoned it. Such a government would be too feeble long to maintain its separate independent existence, and would finally become annexed to or be a dependent colony of some more powerful state. Should any foreign government attempt to possess it as a colony, or otherwise to incorporate it with itself, the principle avowed by President Monroe in 1824, and reaffirmed in my first annual message, that no foreign power shall with our consent be permitted to plant or establish any new colony or dominion on any part of the North American continent must be maintained. In maintaining this principle and in resisting its invasion by any foreign power we might be involved in other wars more expensive and more difficult than that in which we are now engaged. The Provinces of New Mexico and the Californias are contiguous to the territories of the United States, and if brought under the government of our laws their resources—mineral, agricultural, manufacturing, and commercial—would soon be developed.

Upper California is bounded on the north by our Oregon possessions, and if held by the United States would soon be settled by a hardy, enterprising, and intelligent portion of our population. The Bay of San Francisco and other harbors along the Californian coast would afford shelter for our Navy, for our numerous whale ships, and other merchant vessels employed in the Pacific Ocean, and would in a short period become the marts of an extensive and profitable commerce with China and other countries of the East.

These advantages, in which the whole commercial world would participate, would at once be secured to the United States by the cession of this territory; while it is certain that as long as it remains a part of the Mexican dominions they can be enjoyed neither by Mexico herself nor by any other nation.

See *Messages and Papers of the Presidents* (New York: Bureau of National Literature, 1897), 5:2382–414.

Against Polk's Position

HENRY CLAY, SPEECH IN LEXINGTON, KENTUCKY, NOVEMBER 13, 1847

Do we want for our own happiness or greatness the addition of Mexico to the existing Union of our States? If our population was too dense for our territory, and there was a difficulty in obtaining honorably the means of subsistence, there might be some excuse for an attempt to enlarge our dominions. But we have no such apology. We have already, in our glorious country, a vast and almost boundless territory. . . . We have more than ten thousand millions of acres of waste and unsettled lands, enough for the subsistence of ten or twenty times our present population. Ought we not to be satisfied with such a country? Ought we not to be profoundly thankful to the Giver of all good things for such a vast and bountiful land? Is it not the height of ingratitude to Him to seek, by war and conquest, indulging in a spirit of rapacity, to acquire other lands, the homes and habitations of a large portion of his common children?

. . . We do not want the mines, the mountains, the morasses, and the sterile lands of Mexico. To her the loss of them would be humiliating, and be a perpetual source of regret and mortification. To us they might prove a fatal acquisition, producing distraction, dissension, division, possibly disunion. Let, therefore, the integrity of the national existence and national territory of Mexico remain undisturbed. For one, I desire to see no part of her territory torn from her by war. Some of our people have placed their hearts upon the acquisition of the Bay of San Francisco in Upper California. . . . If we can obtain it by fair purchase with a just equivalent, I should be happy to see it so acquired. . . . But it should form no motive in the prosecution of the war, which I would not continue a solitary hour for the sake of that harbor.

See Robert Seager II, ed., *The Papers of Henry Clay*, vol. 10, *Candidate, Compromiser, Elder Statesman* (Lexington: University Press of Kentucky, 1984), 370–71.

OREGON

In addition to California, President Polk was very interested in extending the United States' authority over the whole of the Oregon Territory, which had been co-occupied with Great Britain since 1818. The territory was a large one, reaching from the northern border of Spanish, or Mexican, California at latitude 42° up to the southern border of Russian Alaska at 54° 40'. "Joint Occupation," as it was formally called, did not mean much, really, as in the early years there were few Americans anywhere in the territory save an occasional fur trader here and there, and perhaps an American merchant sailing up the coastline looking for trade. Never was the region entirely out of the minds of American political leaders, though. In 1826, John Quincy Adams engaged in negotiations to build a naval base somewhere along the Oregon coastline. For those interested in encouraging American trade in the Pacific, few anchorages could match that of Puget Sound.

Gradually, however, as Americans pushed westward, more and more funneled into the Oregon country. It was the influx of settlers, more than the interests of politicians, that finally began to tilt the nation firmly in the direction of Oregon. California was the possession of another power, although this did not by any means discourage immigration completely, and Alaska was too far north, but Oregon was a fine, resource-rich territory. By the early 1840s the Oregon Trail had been established from Independence, Missouri, westward as a set route for wagon trains to Oregon. Within a couple of years, there was a significant traffic that eventually grew into a large migration of Americans. In 1843, President Tyler mentioned asserting America's claims to Oregon in expansive terms, and by the time Polk was inaugurated, there were thousands of American settlers living in the fertile valleys of the Willamette and Columbia Rivers. These people wanted the United States to exercise more control over the region, for their own benefit if for no other reason. President Polk, predisposed as he was toward the inevitability of Manifest Destiny and the righteousness of American expansion, decided to force the issue.

Polk loudly claimed that the United States wanted, and would have, all of the Oregon Territory up to Alaska, for which the government was willing to fight if opposed. In his inaugural address, he announced that the U.S. claim to the entire Oregon Territory was "clear and unquestionable." Many who opposed him were convinced that such brash pronouncements by a president would inevitably lead to war with England, something regarded to be irresponsible at best by a lot of people. Polk's claim to the entirety of the territory belied his desire just for the area south of the 49th parallel. He had no desire for all of the Oregon Territory. By no means did he really want 54° 40'. But he realized that a bold claim for all the country could well force the British to negotiate to his position. What he really wanted was Puget Sound. For territory north of there, he could not have cared less.

FROM POLK'S *FIRST ANNUAL MESSAGE TO CONGRESS*, DECEMBER 2, 1845

... My attention was early directed to the negotiation which on the 4th of March last I found pending at Washington between the United States and Great Britain on the subject of the Oregon Territory. Three several attempts had been previously made to settle the questions in dispute between the two countries by negotiation upon the principle of compromise, but each had proved unsuccessful. These negotiations took place at London in the years 1818, 1824, and 1826—the two first under the Administration of Mr. Monroe and the last under that of Mr. Adams. The negotiation of 1818, having failed to accomplish its object, resulted in the convention of the 20th of October of that year.

... When I came into office I found this to be the state of the negotiation. Though entertaining the settled conviction that the British pretensions of title could not be maintained to any portion of the Oregon Territory upon any principle of public law recognized by nations, yet in deference to what had been done by my predecessors ... I deemed it to be my duty not abruptly to break it off. In consideration, too, that under the conventions of 1818 and 1827 the citizens and subjects of the two powers held a joint occupancy of the country, I was induced to make another effort to settle this long-pending controversy in the spirit of moderation which had given birth to the renewed discussion. A proposition was accordingly made, which was rejected by the British plenipotentiary, who, without submitting any other proposition, suffered the negotiation on his part to drop, expressing his trust that the United States would offer what he saw fit to call "some further proposal for the settlement of the Oregon question more consistent with fairness and equity and with the reasonable expectations of the British Government."

... The extraordinary and wholly inadmissible demands of the British Government and the rejection of the proposition made in deference alone to what had been done by my predecessors and the implied obligation which their acts seemed to impose afford satisfactory evidence that no compromise which the United States ought to accept can be effected. With this conviction the proposition of compromise which had been made and rejected was by my direction subsequently withdrawn and our title to the whole Oregon Territory asserted, and, as is believed, maintained by ir-refragable facts and arguments.

The civilized world will see in these proceedings a spirit of liberal con-cession on the part of the United States, and this Government will be re-lieved from all responsibility which may follow the failure to settle the controversy.

All attempts at compromise having failed, it becomes the duty of Con-gress to consider what measures it may be proper to adopt for the secu-rity and protection of our citizens now inhabiting or who may hereafter inhabit Oregon, and for the maintenance of our just title to that Territory. In adopting measures for this purpose care should be taken that nothing be done to violate the stipulations of the convention of 1827, which is still in force. The faith of treaties, in their letter and spirit, has ever been, and, I trust, will ever be, scrupulously observed by the United States. Under that convention a year's notice is required to be given by either party to the other before the joint occupancy shall terminate and before either can rightfully assert or exercise exclusive jurisdiction over any portion of the territory. This notice it would, in my judgment, be proper to give, and I recommend that provision be made by law for giving it accordingly, and terminating in this manner the convention of the 6th of August, 1827.

. . . Beyond all question the protection of our laws and our jurisdiction, civil and criminal, ought to be immediately extended over our citizens in Oregon. They have had just cause to complain of our long neglect in this particular, and have in consequence been compelled for their own secu-rity and protection to establish a provisional government for themselves.

. . . At the end of the year's notice, should Congress think it proper to make provision for giving that notice, we shall have reached a period when the national rights in Oregon must either be abandoned or firmly maintained. That they can not be abandoned without a sacrifice of both national honor and interest is too clear to admit of doubt.

Oregon is a part of the North American continent, to which, it is con-fidently affirmed, the title of the United States is the best now in exis-tence.

See *Messages and Papers of the Presidents* (New York: Bureau of National Literature, 1897), 5:2235–66.

Against Polk's Oregon Position

HENRY CLAY TO JOHN L. LAWRENCE, APRIL 30, 1845

I have all along apprehended that serious difficulty would arise out of the headlong course of our Government in respect to Oregon, at the very

moment when a negotiation is in progress with Great Britain for the settlement of the dispute about that Territory. It has ever appeared to me,
that it was altogether premature to attempt a settlement on the Pacific
Ocean, and assume the consequent duty of its defence, by the requisite
military and naval means, at a time when we have quite enough to defend the coasts of the Atlantic Ocean and the Gulph of Mexico. True wisdom seemed to me to point out, that, whilst we sustained and upheld all
our territorial rights, beyond the Rocky Mountains, we should direct our
present exertions to the increase of population and strength, and the improvement and development of our resources, on this side of those mountains.

. . . I am very apprehensive, my dear sir, that we are shortly to have
war with both England and Mexico. The party in power has not the moral
courage to do right. Polk and Buchanan would never dare settle the question of Oregon without a total surrender on the part of Great Britain of
all her pretensions and she is not going to yield them.

See Robert Seager II, ed., *The Papers of Henry Clay*, vol. 10, *Candidate, Compromiser,
Elder Statesman* (Lexington: University Press of Kentucky, 1984), 223.

THE MEXICAN WAR

Once Texas became part of the United States, it became a duty of the
U.S. government to protect its borders. The question regarding Texas,
however, for which no one seemed to have a definitive answer, was where
exactly that border was. The Mexican government, enraged by the annexation to begin with, insisted that the Nueces River was the border between Texas and Mexico, that is, when it was not insisting that Texas was
still part of Mexico entirely. In the face of the subtly different but equally
determined threats by Mexico to, on the one hand, invade Texas and, on
the other hand, to protect its sovereign territory at all costs, President Polk
sent an army under General Zachary Taylor to the port city of Corpus
Christi, at the mouth of the Nueces River, with orders to be prepared to
defend American soil and interests.

Complicating Polk's diplomacy, and casting every motive and assertion of the president into question, was Polk's desire to bring the Mexican territory of California into the union. Attempts to buy it from Mexico
had come to nothing, but Polk's desire had not flagged. His desire for
California was so well-known among other Washington politicians that
his political opponents began to believe that the president was liable to
use any pretext to go to war with Mexico simply for the purpose of taking California. That Polk's orders to the army to move southward came
immediately on the heels of finding out his overtures to buy California
had come to nothing was enough in most of his detractors' minds to

prove that the two issues were closely related, even though Polk said they were not.

After holding its position along the Nueces for several weeks, Zachary Taylor's army suddenly received orders to move south to the Rio Grande. There, on the north bank—that is, the Texas side—of the river, a small scouting party of the army was attacked by a similar detachment of Mexican soldiers patrolling the north side of the river. Polk seized on this attack, which had clearly taken place, to his eyes and those of the Texans on American soil, as perfect justification for a declaration of war against Mexico. War, moreover, already existed, Polk said. He was only acting in his constitutional authority to defend the United States.

Whig opposition to Polk exploded in Congress. The vagaries of the border situation gave room for the president's more outspoken detractors to claim that the uncertainties of territorial ownership proved that the war was not forced on the president but in fact, cooked up by him as a cover for something else.

FROM POLK TO THE SENATE AND HOUSE OF REPRESENTATIVES, MAY 11, 1846

. . . The strong desire to establish peace with Mexico on liberal and honorable terms, and the readiness of this Government to regulate and adjust our boundary and other causes of difference with that power on such fair and equitable principles as would lead to permanent relations of the most friendly nature, induced me in September last to seek the reopening of diplomatic relations between the two countries. Every measure adopted on our part had for its object the furtherance of these desired results. In communicating to Congress a succinct statement of the injuries which we had suffered from Mexico, and which have been accumulating during a period of more than twenty years, every expression that could tend to inflame the people of Mexico or defeat or delay a pacific result was carefully avoided. An envoy of the United States repaired to Mexico with full powers to adjust every existing difference. But though present on the Mexican soil by agreement between the two Governments, invested with full powers, and bearing evidence of the most friendly dispositions, his mission has been unavailing. The Mexican Government not only refused to receive him or listen to his propositions, but after a long-continued series of menaces have at last invaded our territory and shed the blood of our fellow-citizens on our own soil.

. . . In my message at the commencement of the present session I informed you that upon the earnest appeal both of the Congress and convention of Texas I had ordered an efficient military force to take a position "between the Nueces and the Del Norte." This had become necessary to meet a threatened invasion of Texas by the Mexican forces, for which extensive military preparations had been made. The invasion was threatened solely because Texas had determined, in accordance with a solemn resolution of the Congress of the United States, to annex herself to our Union, and under these circumstances it was plainly our duty to extend our protection over her citizens and soil.

. . . The movement of the troops to the Del Norte was made by the commanding general under positive instructions to abstain from all aggressive acts toward Mexico or Mexican citizens and to regard the relations between that Republic and the United States as peaceful unless she should declare war or commit acts of hostility indicative of a state of war. He was specially directed to protect private property and respect personal rights.

. . . The Mexican forces at Matamoras assumed a belligerent attitude, and on the 12th of April General Ampudia, then in command, notified General Taylor to break up his camp within twenty-four hours and to retire beyond the Nueces River, and in the event of his failure to comply with these demands announced that arms, and arms alone, must decide the question. But no open act of hostility was committed until the 24th of April. On that day General Arista, who had succeeded to the command, of the Mexican forces, communicated to General Taylor that "he considered hostilities commenced and should prosecute them." A party of dragoons of 63 men and officers were on the same day dispatched from the American camp up the Rio del Norte, on its left bank, to ascertain whether the Mexican troops had crossed or were preparing to cross the river, became engaged with a large body of these troops, and after a short affair, in which some 16 were killed and wounded, appear to have been surrounded and compelled to surrender.

. . . The grievous wrongs perpetrated by Mexico upon our citizens throughout a long period of years remain unredressed, and solemn treaties pledging her public faith for this redress have been disregarded. A government either unable or unwilling to enforce the execution of such treaties fails to perform one of its plainest duties.

. . . In the meantime we have tried every effort at reconciliation. The cup of forbearance had been exhausted even before the recent information from the frontier of the Del Norte. But now, after reiterated menaces, Mexico has passed the boundary of the United States, has invaded our territory and shed American blood upon the American soil. She has proclaimed that hostilities have commenced, and that the two nations are now at war.

See *Messages and Papers of the Presidents* (New York: Bureau of National Literature, 1897), 5:2287–93.

Against Polk's Position

REPRESENTATIVE ABRAHAM LINCOLN (WHIG, ILLINOIS), SPEECH IN THE UNITED STATES HOUSE OF REPRESENTATIVES, JANUARY 12, 1848

... When the war began, it way my opinion that all those who ... could not conscientiously approve the conduct of the President, in the beginning of it, should, nevertheless, as good citizens and patriots, remain silent on that point, at least till the war should be ended. Some leading democrats, including Ex President Van Buren, have taken this same view, as I understand them; and I adhered to it, and acted upon it, until since I took my seat here; and I think I should still adhere to it, were it not that the President and his friends will not allow it to be so. Besides the continual effort of the President to argue every silent vote given for supplies, into an endorsement of the justice and wisdom of his conduct ... one of my colleagues ... brought in a set of resolutions, expressly endorsing the original justice of the war on the part of the President. Upon these resolutions ... I can not be silent, if I would. ... I carefully examined the President's messages, to ascertain what he himself had said and proved upon the point. The result of this examination was to make the impression, that taking for true, all the President states as facts, he falls far short of proving his justification; and that the President would have gone farther with his proof, if it had not been for the small matter, that the truth would not permit him. ... I propose now to give, concisely, the process of the examination I made, and how I reached the conclusion I did. The President, in his first war message of May 1846, declares that the soil was ours on which hostilities were commenced by Mexico; and he repeats that declaration, almost in the same language, in each successive annual message, thus showing that he esteems that point, a highly essential one. In the importance of that point, I entirely agree with the President. To my judgment, it is the very point, upon which he should be justified, or condemned. In his message of [December] 1846, it seems to have occurred to him, as is certainly true, that title—ownership—to soil, or any thing else, is not a simple fact; but is a conclusion following one or more simple facts; and that it was incumbent upon him, to present the facts, from which he concluded, the soil was ours, on which the first blood of the war was shed.

... Now I propose to try to show, that the whole of this—issue and evidence—is, from beginning to end, the sheerest deception. The issue, as he presents it, is in these words "but there are those who, conceding all this to be true, assume the ground that the true western boundary of

Texas is the Nueces, instead of the Rio Grande; and that, therefore, in marching our army to the east bank of the latter river, we passed the Texan line, and invaded the territory of Mexico." Now this issue, is made up of two affirmatives and no negative. The main deception of it is, that it assumes as true, that one river or the other is necessarily the boundary; and cheats the superficial thinker entirely out of the idea, that possibly the boundary is somewhere between the two, and not actually at either. A further deception is, that it will let in evidence, which a true issue would exclude. A true issue, made by the President, would be about as follows "I say, the soil was ours, on which the first blood was shed; there are those who say it was not."

   . . . But next the President tells us, the Congress of the United States understood the state of Texas they admitted into the union, to extend beyond the Nueces. Well, I suppose they did. I certainly so understood it. But how far beyond? That Congress did not understand it to extend clear to the Rio Grande, is quite certain by the fact of their joint resolutions, for admission, expressly leaving all questions of boundary to future adjustment. And it may be added, that Texas herself, is proved to have had the same understanding of it, that our Congress had, by the fact of the exact conformity of her new constitution, to those resolutions.

   . . . Now sir, for the purpose of obtaining the very best evidence, as to whether Texas had actually carried her revolution, to the place where the hostilities of the present war commenced, let the President answer the interrogatories, I proposed, as before mentioned, or some other similar ones. Let him answer, fully, fairly, and candidly. Let him answer with facts, and not with arguments. Let him remember he sits where Washington sat, and so remembering, let him answer, as Washington would answer. As a nation should not, and the Almighty will not, be evaded, so let him attempt no evasion—no equivocation. And if, so answering, he can show that the soil was ours, where the first blood of the war was shed—that it was not within an inhabited country, or, if within such, that the inhabitants had submitted themselves to the civil authority of Texas, or of the United States, and that the same is true of the site of Fort Brown, then I am with him for his justification. In that case I, shall be most happy to reverse the vote I gave the other day. I have a selfish motive for desiring that the President may do this. I expect to give some votes, in connection with the war, which, without his so doing, will be of doubtful propriety in my own judgment, but which will be free from the doubt if he does so. But if he can not, or will not do this—if on any pretence, or no pretence, he shall refuse or omit it, then I shall be fully convinced, of what I more than suspect already, that he is deeply conscious of being in the wrong—that he feels the blood of this war, like the blood of Abel, is crying to Heaven against him.

See Roy P. Basler, ed., *Collected Works of Abraham Lincoln*, vol. 1 (Springfield, Ill.: The Abraham Lincoln Association; New Brunswick, N.J.: Rutgers University Press, 1953).

THE TARIFF

One of Polk's intentions in running for president was to reduce the tariff. Like every other Democrat, Polk opposed the notion of a protective tariff. He marshaled no new arguments against the policy, but made it clear that he would block with all his authority any attempts to raise it or make it more openly protective. The sizable majority in the House of Representatives, where Democrats outnumbered Whigs 143 to 77, provided the Polk administration a considerable amount of influence to shape the tariff issue to his liking. Treasury Secretary Robert Walker did a considerable amount of research on what was the lowest level at which the administration could set the tariff and still generate enough funds for the government to meet its obligations. All the incremental increases that had crept into tariff policy since the Compromise Tariff of 1833, changes codified in the Tariff of 1842, were to be purged and the rates set at least as low as they had been in that legislation.

The House complied readily and produced a bill that became known as the Walker Tariff, significantly reducing rates on almost all imports. In the Senate, the Democrat majority was much less, but the result was eventually the same. Polk became personally involved in the debates, never hesitating to use the influence of the presidency. The result was a low tariff that remained in place until the late 1850s. More importantly from a political standpoint, the establishment of the Walker Tariff removed the issue of tariffs from political debate for years. Consequently, Congress would fight over other issues instead.

Once again, Henry Clay stalwartly defended the policy of protection of which he had so long been an ardent advocate. Excessively low tariff levels not only failed to offer domestic industries protection from cheap imports; they even jeopardized the fiscal stability of the nation. Low tariff levels meant less revenue, and less of a cushion in times in which unexpected spending was necessary. Clay and others fully expected that government revenues would plummet to a dangerously low level, bringing all sorts of additional economic trouble if the tariff was set lower than the 1842 level.

FROM POLK'S *THIRD ANNUAL MESSAGE TO CONGRESS*, DECEMBER 7, 1847

. . . The act of the 30th of July, 1846, "reducing the duties on imports," has been in force since the 1st of December last, and I am gratified to state that all the beneficial effects which were anticipated from its operation have been fully realized. The public revenue derived from customs during the year ending on the 1st of December, 1847, exceeds by more than $8,000,000 the amount received in the preceding year under the operation of the act of 1842, which was superseded and repealed by it. Its effects are visible in the great and almost unexampled prosperity which prevails in every branch of business.

While the repeal of the prohibitory and restrictive duties of the act of 1842 and the substitution in their place of reasonable revenue rates levied on articles imported according to their actual value has increased the revenue and augmented our foreign trade, all the great interests of the country have been advanced and promoted.

The great and important interests of agriculture, which had been not only too much neglected, but actually taxed under the protective policy for the benefit of other interests, have been relieved of the burdens which that policy imposed on them; and our farmers and planters, under a more just and liberal commercial policy, are finding new and profitable markets abroad for their augmented products. Our commerce is rapidly increasing, and is extending more widely the circle of international exchanges. Great as has been the increase of our imports during the past year, our exports of domestic products sold in foreign markets have been still greater.

Our navigating interest is eminently prosperous. The number of vessels built in the United States has been greater than during any preceding period of equal length. Large profits have been derived by those who have constructed as well as by those who have navigated them. Should the ratio of increase in the number of our merchant vessels be progressive, and be as great for the future as during the past year, the time is not distant when our tonnage and commercial marine will be larger than that of any other nation in the world.

Whilst the interests of agriculture, of commerce, and of navigation have been enlarged and invigorated, it is highly gratifying to observe that our manufactures are also in a prosperous condition. None of the ruinous effects upon this interest which were apprehended by some as the result of the operation of the revenue system established by the act of 1846 have been experienced. On the contrary, the number of manufactories and the amount of capital invested in them is steadily and rapidly increasing, affording gratifying proofs that American enterprise and skill employed in this branch of domestic industry, with no other advantages than those fairly and incidentally accruing from a just System of revenue duties, are abundantly able to meet successfully all competition from abroad and still derive fair and remunerating profits. While capital invested in manufactures is yielding adequate and fair profits under the new system, the wages of labor, whether employed in manufactures, agriculture, commerce, or navigation, have been augmented. The toiling millions whose daily labor furnishes the supply of food and raiment and all the necessaries and comforts of life are receiving higher wages and more steady and permanent employment than in any other country or at any previous period of our own history.

See *Messages and Papers of the Presidents* (New York: Bureau of National Literature, 1897), 5:2382–414.

Against Polk's Position

HENRY CLAY TO JOHN M. CLAYTON, AUGUST 22, 1844

The people of 1842, the Whigs at least every where, and many of the Democrats, are now fully persuaded that the industry of this great Country ought not to be prostrated at the feet of Foreign powers. Every where the cry is for a Tariff of Revenue, with discriminations for protection. Every where the preservation of the Tariff of 1842, which has worked so well, and is delivering us from embarrassments, is loudly demanded.

[Now, however,] the great, practical, absorbing question is shall the Tariff of 1842 be preserved or repealed? That question is to be solved in November next. I have repeatedly expressed my opinion, unequivocally, in favor of it.

I thought we achieved a great triumph in placing the Protective policy, by the Compromise act, without the reach and beyond the term of Genl. Jackson's administration. And we availed ourselves of the fact that the South Carolina delegation were much more anxious that the difficulty should be settled by us than by Genl. Jackson.

You tell me that I am accused of having abandoned the Protective policy. That would distress me exceedingly, if I were not accused of all sorts of crimes and misdemeanors. . . . I laugh at the streights to which our opponents are driven. They are to be pitied. Shrinking from all the issues, arising out of the great questions of National policy, which have hitherto divided the Country, they have no other refuge left but in personal abuse, detraction and defamation. . . . Most certainly my surprise at the attempt to make me out a friend of free trade with Foreign Countries, and an opponent of the Protective policy, ought not to be greater than that of my Competitor [Polk] at the effort to establish his friendship to the Protective policy.

See Robert Seager II, ed., *The Papers of Henry Clay*, vol. 10, *Candidate, Compromiser, Elder Statesman* (Lexington: University Press of Kentucky, 1984), 101–2.

SLAVERY

Abolitionist rhetoric was getting hotter and hotter by the middle of the 1840s. Just two months after James K. Polk took office, Frederick Douglass's autobiography was published. In gripping detail, the book related the struggles of his life as a slave and the inhuman treatment he had received at the hands of various masters before escaping to freedom. In abolitionist circles, the book was a bombshell. There had been numerous other such accounts penned by runaway slaves, but Douglass's had a clarity and eloquence like no other. After its publication, and fearing for his safety, Douglass fled the United States for two years. During this time, he traveled throughout Europe giving speeches and raising money for the cause. When he came back, he was nothing short of a celebrity, and became a moving and persuasive spokesman for the cause of abolition. He traveled tirelessly all around New England, often in the company of William Lloyd Garrison, giving speeches to packed halls and anti-slavery societies from city to city. The same year his book was published in the United States, it came out in Europe, and this, combined with Douglass's time on the other side of the Atlantic, made both sides of the issue aware that the eyes of abolitionists throughout the world were increasingly turned to slavery in the American South. More people were joining the abolitionist cause, and it seemed as though a neutral position on the issue was getting increasingly difficult to maintain. Northern states, starting with Massachusetts in 1842, passed laws forbidding state officials to help capture runaway slaves. Within five years six states had such laws on the books. More and more, abolitionists, and even those politicians who considered themselves friends of the abolitionist cause, were unwilling to remain quiet on the issue. The question of slavery had become an utterly moral cause to those who opposed it, with no shades of gray. It was simply an abhorrent wrong and if one was not actively against it, he was helping it continue.

But as loud and as dedicated as the abolitionists were becoming, so too were the defenders of slavery increasingly unwilling to be quiet, especially when confronted by the fervor of abolitionists. Throughout states closer to the South, outspoken abolitionists and newspaper editors were assaulted and sometimes killed. Mobs in southern cities burned bags of mail if they thought there might be abolitionist literature inside. Preachers and others who dared to speak out against slavery found themselves run out of town. As the two positions radicalized, there was less and less middle ground to occupy. The issue had reached the point at which it was not going to recede from public discourse and argument. It would never be as quiescent as it once was.

Quiet, however, was what Polk and many other national politicians who defended the institution wanted and expected. It had been informal policy for years now that slavery was to be kept out of public discourse. In his inaugural address, Polk made it clear that that is what he wanted to continue. If the two main parties were going to keep the issue off the table, opponents of slavery would form their own party. The Liberty Party in 1844 was the result. The platform of the new Liberty Party in the 1844 campaign illustrated the growing impatience of abolitionists and showed the willingness to force slavery into the center of American politics.

FROM POLK'S *INAUGURAL ADDRESS*, MARCH 4, 1845

. . . Every lover of his country must shudder at the thought of the possibility of its dissolution, and will be ready to adopt the patriotic sentiment, "Our Federal Union—it must be preserved." To preserve it the compromises which alone enabled our fathers to form a common constitution for the government and protection of so many States and distinct communities, of such diversified habits, interests, and domestic institutions, must be sacredly and religiously observed. Any attempt to disturb or destroy these compromises, being terms of the compact of union, can lead to none other than the most ruinous and disastrous consequences.

It is a source of deep regret that in some sections of our country misguided persons have occasionally indulged in schemes and agitations whose object is the destruction of domestic institutions existing in other sections—institutions which existed at the adoption of the Constitution and were recognized and protected by it. All must see that if it were possible for them to be successful in attaining their object the dissolution of the Union and the consequent destruction of our happy form of government must speedily follow.

I am happy to believe that at every period of our existence as a nation there has existed, and continues to exist, among the great mass of our people a devotion to the Union of the States which will shield and protect it against the moral treason of any who would seriously contemplate its destruction. To secure a continuance of that devotion the compromises of the Constitution must not only be preserved, but sectional jealousies and heartburnings must be discountenanced, and all should remember that they are members of the same political family, having a common destiny.

See *Messages and Papers of the Presidents* (New York: Bureau of National Literature, 1897), 5:2223–32.

Against Polk's Position

FROM THE PLATFORM OF THE LIBERTY PARTY, 1844

13. Resolved, That the provision of the Constitution of the United States, which confers extraordinary political powers on the owners of slaves, and thereby constituting the two hundred and fifty thousand slaveholders in the slave States a privileged aristocracy; and the provision for the reclamation of fugitive slaves from service, are anti-republican in their character, dangerous to the liberties of the people, and ought to be abrogated.

14. Resolved, That the operation of the first of these provisions is seen in the growth of a power in the country, hostile to free institutions, to free labor, and to freedom itself, which is appropriately denominated the slave power; this power has maintained slavery in the original States, has secured its continuance in the District and in the Territories, has created seven new slave States, has caused fluctuations in our national policy, foreign and domestic, has gradually usurped the control of our home legislation, has waged unrelenting war against the most sacred rights of freedom, has violated and set at naught the right of petition, has dictated the action of political parties, has filled almost all the offices of the National Government with slaveholders, and the abettors of slaveholders, and threatens, if not arrested in its career, the total overthrow of popular freedom.

16. Resolved, That the peculiar patronage and support hitherto extended to slavery and slaveholding, by the General Government, ought to be immediately withdrawn, and the example and influence of national authority ought to be arrayed on the side of Liberty and free labor.

17. Resolved, That we cherish no harsh or unkind feelings towards any of our brethren of the slave States, while we express unmitigated abhorrence of that system of slaveholding which has stripped a large portion of their population of every right, and which has established an aristocracy worse than feudal in the midst of Republican States, and which denies to the poor non-slaveholder and his children the benefits of education, and crushes them in the dust, or drives them out as exiles from the land of their birth.

See Arthur M. Schlesinger Jr. et al., *History of American Presidential Elections, 1789–1968* (New York: Chelsea House, 1971), 2:816–17.

THE "INDEPENDENT TREASURY"

Whigs in Congress had passed legislation repealing the Independent Treasury early in John Tyler's administration, and Tyler had signed it into law. Since then, government funds had been regularly deposited in a series of state banks. Polk, however, was determined to resurrect the idea of an independent storehouse for the government's money and was worried that the longer such an independent institution did not exist, the more support would begin to gather for a return to a national bank. Many Democrats in Congress shared this worry, and were receptive to Polk's resuscitating the Independent Treasury plan.

Again, Secretary Walker was instrumental in shaping Polk's ideas for presentation in Congress. The administration planned to construct enormous fireproof vaults in Washington, D.C., in which government funds would be kept in secure isolation. House Democrats, hearkening back to the policy of the later days of the Jackson administration, added an amendment to guarantee that all government transactions would be carried on using specie only—gold or silver—and not paper notes. Such a policy would ensure that the worth of the government's money was solid and guard against currency inflation that so undermined the country's economic stability.

By the time of Polk's administration and his well-known backing of the sub-treasury plan, the opposition to the measure was not bringing forward any new particulars in its opposition to it. It was becoming more wrapped up in the Whig opposition to the general way the Democrat party operated and to its overall platform. Clay's opinion of it in 1844 is clear by looking at the policies with which he associates it. By the end of Polk's term, with the sub-treasury in place, Clay's opposition sounds more weary and resigned. There are two reasons for this. First of all, Clay himself was growing older and wearier of the fight. Second, and perhaps more importantly for rhetorical reasons, other issues were beginning to eclipse something at the same time so financially obtuse and so very mundane as debates and arguments over the particulars of the country's financial system. Those other issues involved slavery and how to manage the new territories gained via the Mexican War.

The success enjoyed by Polk in getting the Independent Treasury created took the issue out of politics for decades. It would not be until the next century that Congress reassessed its treasury policy.

FROM POLK'S *FIRST ANNUAL MESSAGE TO CONGRESS*, DECEMBER 2, 1845

... A public treasury was undoubtedly contemplated and intended to be created [by the Founders], in which the public money should be kept from the period of collection until needed for public uses. In the collection and disbursement of the public money no agencies have ever been employed by law except such as were appointed by the Government, directly responsible to it and under its control. The safe-keeping of the public money should be confided to a public treasury created by law and under like responsibility and control. It is not to be imagined that the framers of the Constitution could have intended that a treasury should be created as a place of deposit and safe-keeping of the public money which was irresponsible to the Government. . . . That banks, national or State, could not have been intended to be used as a substitute for the Treasury spoken of in the Constitution as keepers of the public money is manifest from the fact that at that time there was no national bank, and but three or four State banks, of limited capital, existed in the country. Their employment as depositories was at first resorted to a limited extent, but with no avowed intention of continuing them permanently in place of the Treasury of the Constitution. When they were afterwards from time to time employed, it was from motives of supposed convenience. Our experience has shown that when banking corporations have been the keepers of the public money, and been thereby made in effect the Treasury, the Government can have no guaranty that it can command the use of its own money for public purposes. The late Bank of the United States proved to be faithless. The State banks which were afterwards employed were faithless. But a few years ago, with millions of public money in their keeping, the Government was brought almost to bankruptcy and the public credit seriously impaired because of their inability or indisposition to pay on demand to the public creditors in the only currency recognized by the Constitution. Their failure occurred in a period of peace, and great inconvenience and loss were suffered by the public from it. Had the country been involved in a foreign war, that inconvenience and loss would have been much greater, and might have resulted in extreme public calamity. The public money should not be mingled with the private funds of banks or individuals or be used for private purposes. When it is placed in banks for safe-keeping, it is in effect loaned to them without interest, and is loaned by them upon interest to the borrowers from them. . . . The framers of the Constitution could never have intended that the money paid into the Treasury should be thus converted to private use and placed beyond the control of the Government.

Banks which hold the public money are often tempted by a desire of gain to extend their loans, increase their circulation, and thus stimulate, if not produce, a spirit of speculation and extravagance which sooner or later must result in ruin to thousands. If the public money be not permitted to be thus used, but be kept in the Treasury and paid out to the public creditors in gold and silver, the temptation afforded by its deposit with banks to an undue expansion of their business would be checked, while the amount of the constitutional currency left in circulation would be enlarged by its employment in the public collections and disbursements, and the banks themselves would in consequence be found in a safer and sounder condition.

. . . Entertaining the opinion that "the separation of the moneys of the Government from banking institutions is indispensable for the safety of the funds of the Government and the rights of the people," I recommend to Congress that provision be made by law for such separation, and that a constitutional treasury be created for the safe-keeping of the public money. . . . I can not doubt that such a treasury as was contemplated by the Constitution should be independent of all banking corporations. The money of the people should be kept in the Treasury of the people created by law, and be in the custody of agents of the people chosen by themselves according to the forms of the Constitution—agents who are directly responsible to the Government, who are under adequate bonds and oaths, and who are subject to severe punishments for any embezzlement, private use, or misapplication of the public funds, and for any failure in other respects to perform their duties. To say that the people or their Government are incompetent or not to be trusted with the custody of their own money in their own Treasury, provided by themselves, but must rely on the presidents, cashiers, and stockholders of banking corporations, not appointed by them nor responsible to them, would be to concede that they are incompetent for self-government.

See *Messages and Papers of the Presidents* (New York: Bureau of National Literature, 1897), 5:2235–66.

Against Polk's Position

HENRY CLAY, SPEECH IN RALEIGH, NORTH CAROLINA, APRIL 13, 1844

The Whigs believe that the Executive power has, during the two last and the present administration, been intolerably abused; that it has disturbed the balances of the Constitution; and that, by its encroachments upon the co-ordinate branches of the Government, it has become alarming and dangerous. . . . But our opponents, who assume to be emphatically the friends of the people, sustain the Executive in all its wildest and most extravagant excesses. They go for Vetoes in all their vanity, for Subtreasuries, standing armies, treasury circulars! Occupying a similar ground with the Tories of England, they stand up for power and prerogative against . . . popular rights.

See Robert Seager II, ed., *The Papers of Henry Clay*, vol. 10, *Candidate, Compromiser, Elder Statesman* (Lexington: University Press of Kentucky, 1984), 10.

HENRY CLAY TO EPES SARGENT, FEBRUARY 15, 1847

. . . You might draw a strong contrast between the actual condition of the Country now, under Mr. Polk's administration, and what it would have been if the Whigs had prevailed [in the election of 1844]. In the latter event, there would have been no annexation of Texas, no war with Mexico, no National debt, no repeal of the Tariff of 1842, no Sub-treasury, no imputation against us, by the united voice of all the nations of the earth, of a spirit of aggression and inordinate Territorial aggrandizement. But I forebear.

See Robert Seager II, ed., *The Papers of Henry Clay*, vol. 10, *Candidate, Compromiser, Elder Statesman* (Lexington: University Press of Kentucky, 1984), 308.

RECOMMENDED READINGS

Bergeron, Paul H. *The Presidency of James K. Polk*. Lawrence: University Press of Kansas, 1987.

Graebner, Norman. *Empire on the Pacific*. Reprint ed. Claremont, Calif.: Regina Books, 1983.

Holt, Michael F. *The Rise and Fall of the American Whig Party*. New York: Oxford University Press, 1999.

Leonard, Thomas M. *James K. Polk: A Clear and Unquestionable Destiny*. Wilmington, Del.: SR Books, 2001.

Pletcher, David M. *The Diplomacy of Annexation: Texas, Oregon, and the Mexican War*. Columbia: University of Missouri Press, 1975.

BIBLIOGRAPHY

Bemis, Samuel F. *A Diplomatic History of the United States.* 4th ed. New York: Holt, 1955.

———. *John Quincy Adams and the Union.* New York: Knopf, 1965.

Bergeron, Paul H. *The Presidency of James K. Polk.* Lawrence: University Press of Kansas, 1987.

Clarfield, Gerard. *United States Diplomatic History.* Vol. I, *From Revolution to Empire.* Englewood Cliffs, N.J.: Prentice Hall, 1992.

Cole, Donald B. *The Presidency of Andrew Jackson.* Lawrence: University Press of Kansas, 1993.

Dangerfield, George. *The Awakening of American Nationalism.* New York: Harper & Row, 1965.

———. *The Era of Good Feelings.* Chicago: Ivan R. Dee, 1952.

Freehling, William W. *Prelude to Civil War: The Nullification Controversy in South Carolina, 1816–1836.* New York: Harper & Row, 1966.

Graebner, Norman. *Empire on the Pacific.* Reprint ed. Claremont, Calif.: Regina Books, 1983.

Hargreaves, Mary W. M. *The Presidency of John Quincy Adams.* Lawrence: University Press of Kansas, 1985.

Holt, Michael F. *The Rise and Fall of the American Whig Party.* New York: Oxford University Press, 1999.

Leonard, Thomas M. *James K. Polk: A Clear and Unquestionable Destiny.* Wilmington, Del.: SR Books, 2001.

McDonald, Forrest. *States' Rights and the Union:* Imperium in Imperio, *1776–1876.* Lawrence: University Press of Kansas, 2000.

Merk, Frederick. *Manifest Destiny and Mission in American History: A Reinterpretation.* Cambridge, Mass.: Harvard University Press, 1963.

Monroe, Dan. *The Republican Vision of John Tyler.* College Station: Texas A&M University Press, 2003.

Mushkat, Jerome, and Joseph G. Rayback. *Martin Van Buren: Law, Politics, and the Shaping of Republican Ideology*. DeKalb: Northern Illinois University Press, 1997.

Nagel, Paul C. *John Quincy Adams: A Public Life, a Private Life*. Cambridge, Mass.: Harvard University Press, 1999.

Niven, John. *Martin Van Buren: The Romantic Age of American Politics*. New York: Oxford University Press, 1983.

Peterson, Merrill D. *The Great Triumvirate: Webster, Clay, and Calhoun*. New York: Oxford University Press, 1987.

Peterson, Norma Lois. *The Presidencies of William Henry Harrison and John Tyler*. Lawrence: University Press of Kansas, 1989.

Pletcher, David M. *The Diplomacy of Annexation: Texas, Oregon, and the Mexican War*. Columbia: University of Missouri Press, 1975.

Remini, Robert V. *Andrew Jackson and the Bank War*. New York: W. W. Norton & Co., 1967.

———. *The Life of Andrew Jackson*. New York: Harper & Row, 1988.

———. *Martin Van Buren and the Making of the Democratic Party*. New York: Columbia University Press, 1959.

Schlesinger, Arthur M., Jr. *The Age of Jackson*. Boston: Little, Brown & Co., 1953.

Seager, Robert, II. *And Tyler, Too*. New York: McGraw-Hill, 1963.

Sellers, Charles. *The Market Revolution: Jacksonian America, 1815–1846*. New York: Oxford University Press, 1991.

Silbey, Joel H. *Martin Van Buren and the Emergence of Popular American Politics*. Lanham, Md.: Rowman and Littlefield, 2002.

Smith, Henry Nash. *Virgin Land: The American West as Symbol and Myth*. Cambridge, Mass.: Harvard University Press, 1950, 1978.

Wilson, Major L. *The Presidency of Martin Van Buren*. Lawrence: University Press of Kansas, 1984.

INDEX

About the Author

DAVID A. SMITH is Lecturer, Department of History, Baylor University, Waco, Texas. He is the author of *George S. Patton: A Biography* (Greenwood, 2003).